The Impossible:

tracking Luke's gospel

John Bloor

GILEΛD

B O O K S

Gilead Books Publishing
Corner Farm
West Knapton
Malton
North Yorkshire YO17 8JB
www.GileadBooks.com

First published in Great Britain, September 2010
2 4 6 8 10 9 7 5 3 1

Copyright © John Bloor 2010

British Library Cataloguing-in-Publication Data:
A catalogue record for this book is available from the British Library.

ISBN-13: 978-0-9558099-8-9

The publisher makes every effort to ensure that the papers used in our books
are made from trees that have been legally sourced from well-managed and
credibly certified forests by using a printer awarded FSC & PEFC chain of
custody certification.

Illustrations: ©Anna Tash
Cover design: Dave Magill
Editor: David Burton
Graphics: Joanna Hayes

Mixed Sources
Product group from well-managed
forests, and other controlled sources
www.fsc.org Cert no. TT-COC-002641
© 1996 Forest Stewardship Council
FSC

To Sally

CONTENTS

Part Four: Jerusalem

FOREWORD

If you don't know the Gospel story well you should read this book! John Bloor brings Luke's story of Jesus alive, showing its relevance for today, and how it has spoken into his own life.

And if you think you do know the Gospel story well, you should still read this book. You may discover things you had not noticed.

Highly recommended.

Bishop Graham Cray
Archbishops' Missioner

PREFACE

The aim of this book is to bring the gospel of Luke to twenty-first century readers, and to open minds to the sheer delight of the gospel, as well as provoking thought into deep questions. We start by recognising that no one can have a relationship with God - but the excitement of Luke's gospel is that it shows us how Jesus changed that, and gave us what we could never achieve. How Jesus made the impossible possible.

The Impossible tracks Luke's gospel chapter by chapter. By no stretch of the imagination can this book be described as a commentary. It doesn't set out to deal with everything contained in Luke's enduring work. Neither does it lay claim to any scholarly merits. I am an ordinary Christian, and this book is my interpretation of Luke's gospel, drawing on my experience, and how I have found it particularly relevant to my life. The intention is to spark in you the same interest and enthusiasm that this gospel inspires in me, and to provide a possible stepping-stone for others to dig deeper into intellectual writing and investigation of the gospels as a whole.

This is a book that shows how Jesus is so relevant to the problems that face us now in the workplace, at home and in the church. I have unashamedly made use of imagination. With imagination we can look at how Jesus might have told his parables to us if he was telling them today, and perhaps how our conversations with Jesus might have gone had we been alongside him, walking and speaking with him on his way to Jerusalem. It is not hard to see ourselves in many of the people that Jesus met on the way. In their grief we can recall our grief, in their frustration we can recognise our frustrations, in their joy we can rejoice with what make us laugh. Readers may find that this personal interpretation fits alongside theirs or they may add their own variance to it; but either way, this is a book essentially to be enjoyed, because Jesus was and is an enjoyable person to be with.

The Impossible can be read as a stand-alone book or it could be read side by side with the text of the gospel. It is for anyone enquiring, beginning or developing their Christian faith but it might also appeal to those who are far less familiar with Jesus of Nazareth. The chapters also might form the basis for group discussion.

John Bloor
Chatham, 2010

ACKNOWLEDGEMENTS

I would like to thank the following for their love and support given to me during the time it took to write this book through to publication.

Bishop Graham who wrote the Foreword. My Christian life began in the same 'cradle' as Bishop Graham so he seemed the obvious person to ask to write this.

Gilead Books, the publishers, particularly to Chris Hayes for all his support and also, David Burton (Editor), Dave Magill (Cover), Anna Tash (Illustrations) and Joanna Hayes (Graphics)

My church in Chatham, Kent. It's a Local Ecumenical Partnership which means that we are Church of England, Baptist and United Reform all working together.

I have a support group; Chris Green, Ernie and Janet Mann, George and Julia Hulme, Carol and Andy Ward. Many thanks for their prayers and practical support

My ex-colleagues at work, Adrian Rose and Julia White, who read the chapters as I wrote them and encouraged me particularly when I was flagging.

I also want to thank a group of people who generously agreed to read the first drafts and whose feedback determined the road to publication. Amongst those I would mention Dr Paul Wright, who has commended this book and who has been a great strength first as my parish priest in years gone by and later as a dear friend. Professor Chris Cook set me right over a number of matters and Dr Russ Rook who took time to comment and commend. I pray for God's strength for him as he continues his work with Chapel Street. David Smith, who also wrote a commendation, was amongst my first mentors in the Christian faith. This book bought me back into contact with him again.

Finally, a most special thanks and acknowledgement to Sally, my wife, friend and soul-mate. Without her, this book would have not happened.

John Bloor

BETHLEHEM

She was sitting alone on the pavement and it was dark. She was alone because she couldn't go any further. Her companion had gone off by himself to find somewhere, just somewhere, that they might stay. Although alone, there were many people in Bethlehem that night also trying to find somewhere to stay. As they passed her by, some would glance at her sitting undignified, her back propped against a wall and her tummy swollen with advanced expectancy.

'I do hope that he finds somewhere soon,' she thought. 'God,' she spoke out into the darkness, 'couldn't this have happened some other time?'

She thought back over that long journey from her home in Nazareth to Bethlehem with Joseph, the man that she was to marry. The journey was a tough one, even for the fittest, but it was a veritable ordeal for one in the last stages of pregnancy. 'It would have been a bit easier if we had had a donkey' she thought, still speaking to God. 'A donkey? We can't afford a donkey,' she laughed, quietly trying to amuse herself within her own reflections.

But the worst part of the journey came at the end when, exhausted as she was, she had had to haul herself up the steep slope that led into Bethlehem.

With tears in her eyes she lifted her face to the sky:

> *My soul glorifies the Lord*
> *and my spirit rejoices in God my saviour,*
> *for he has been mindful*
> *of the humble state of his servant.*
> *From now on all generations will call me blessed,*
> *for the Mighty One has done great things for me-*
> *holy is his name.*
> *(Luke 1: 46-49)*

'I do hope he finds somewhere soon,' she repeated, and through the night came a familiar figure. It was Joseph - his face concerned but his hands outstretched, and a smile on his young face. She forced herself up once more, hoping above all that the place he had found for them to stay was comfortable and clean.

Part One: Birth

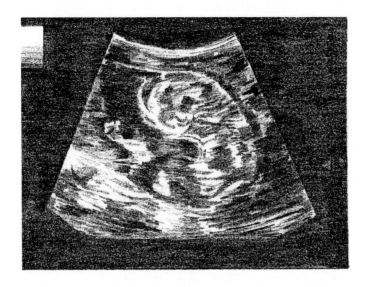

CHAPTER 1

NOTHING IS IMPOSSIBLE WITH GOD

...to shine on those living in darkness... (Luke 1:79)

My dad had a problem with God. I suppose you could say that about all of us, one way or another. However, my dad's problem wasn't about whether he believed in God, but rather whether God believed in him. As I listened to my dad, I could see his point of view. He would, 'just think of God for a moment. God is very big and I am very small by comparison. If God is so big, how can he possibly have any relationship with me? It would be like having a relationship with a speck'. What he was saying, in his own way, is something I have heard from several different people. They point out that, if God exists at all, then we can't be remotely in the same league as him.

Although my dad had a point, he could never get beyond it. The problem, as he saw it, blocked any further investigation. In the end I wondered whether the problem only served as an excuse to look no further. It became an old chestnut to be wheeled out should the subject of God ever be raised. My dad was a wealthy man, in a professional, middle-class way, and I don't think he saw any real need for God; so it was convenient for him to have this 'problem'. After all, a search for God might produce something unexpected and, when things are generally good, the unexpected might turn out to be something unwelcome.

So I began to write this book remembering the conversations that I had with my dad. I have held in mind all those who are like me, who want to know about God, and start out each day seeking to travel further into the faith we have found – whether recently or a long time ago. But I have also held in mind all those who don't believe in God at all, or perhaps are not sure about God and prefer, like my dad, not to search for answers. My dad died some years ago, but I know that he would have wanted to read this book. So if it can't be read by my dad, perhaps it can be read by those who, in spite of their various misgivings about God, are open-minded enough to look at the possibilities.

Those conversations with my dad were always very pleasant, as we shared our varied life experiences. I think that my dad, if he had given himself the opportunity, would have enjoyed the gospel written by a man called Luke whose ambition was to tell us about Jesus, the most amazing person who has ever walked this planet. Like Luke, I want to bring what I have experienced and witnessed into this living gospel, in order to see the relevance of Jesus in our time. I have therefore tracked the gospel of Luke chapter by chapter, giving a personal interpretation of the events recorded there.

But first, a brief look at the author of Luke's gospel. Commentators think that Luke was born in Antioch, which is now in modern day Turkey, and he is thought to have died at the ripe old age of 84 in Boeotia, Greece. He wrote both this gospel and its sequel, 'The Acts of the Apostles'. He was a physician or doctor by profession - which is a very important fact about him, particularly when we read what he came to write about the characteristics of the risen body of Jesus (see chapter twenty-four). But the most important thing about Luke for me is what he wrote right at the beginning of the gospel:

...I myself have carefully investigated everything from the beginning, I too decided to write an orderly account for you. (Luke 1:3)

Luke may not have been an eyewitness to the ministry of Jesus, but he was very active within the ministry of the Apostles that followed the death and resurrection of Jesus. Luke wanted to investigate. He wasn't prepared to stop with the questions. He wanted answers - to know how it is possible for the creator-God to have any sort of relationship with us, or whether there is a heaven or a paradise after death; and we find the answers to these questions and others in his gospel.

In my imagination, if I were to meet Luke, I would ask him why he wrote the gospel in the first place. I think that he would give me two reasons. The first would be to tell Jesus' story. The second would be to convince anybody reading it that the only way that we will find God is through the way that God designed. So let us start from where we are as we follow Luke's gospel.

Nothing is impossible with God

Near the beginning of Luke's gospel there is a very familiar verse loved by Christians, which says 'for nothing is impossible with God' (Luke 1:37, NIV). The sentiment is repeated later in chapter eighteen - 'what is impossible with human beings is possible with God' (Luke 18:27). Christians love these verses because they bring comfort in a tough world full of disappointments, worries and problems. Financial distress? Nothing is impossible with God. Diagnosed with a life threatening illness? But nothing is impossible with God! Some churches display banners with this verse blazoned out for all to see, maintaining this faith in God who created all things.

However, we might look at this verse in the context that it was said, in chapter one. The angel Gabriel was sent by God to the Virgin Mary before the birth of Jesus. Mary saw the angel and was, quite naturally, frightened out of her wits. The angel told her firstly not to be afraid and then secondly that she was going to give birth to a son.

Mary was terrified but not stupid. She was well aware of what it took to become pregnant, and she also knew that what it took to become pregnant hadn't happened. However, instead of shooing the intruder out, she asked how this would be possible and, in reply, the angel told her that the father of the child would be God and that she would become pregnant through the Holy Spirit of God. The angel's explanation finished with the well-known quotation 'for nothing is impossible with God.'

So the context of this statement is not as all-embracing as we might like to think it is. It would seem, on the face of it, to be said specifically to Mary about the circumstances of her forthcoming pregnancy. But it goes beyond this because the baby to be born, to be called Jesus, was to be the very means whereby all people can have a relationship with God. 'How will this be?' (Luke 1:34) asked Mary to the angel about her pregnancy, and we might ask the same question. Is this possible? Is it really possible for God to have and want a relationship with me? 'Nothing is impossible with God,' said the angel about the birth of Jesus, and Luke centres his gospel around impossibility made possible.

But Mary wasn't the first person that the angel had visited before the birth of Jesus.

Zachariah

Zachariah was a priest in the mid-to-late years of his life, married to Elizabeth. In spite of his calling, poor Zachariah and his wife lived in spiritual darkness because their lives were blighted by a frustrated aspiration. In fact, more accurately, their hopes and dreams lay in wreckage. What they wanted so much was a child. They had lived their lives in hope but now it was too late, for they had grown too old. It seemed that their longed-for aspiration was never going to happen. Zachariah had prayed to God but his heart-felt prayers had faded away as he wondered whether God was there at all.

Zachariah and Elizabeth represent all ordinary people who are struggling to find their deepest desires. They represent all who have frustrated aspirations. Perhaps it is to find our dream partner, to have a family, to sit in front of a roaring fire with slippers and a dog. Perhaps it is to develop our talents and to find fame, or to travel the world. Or perhaps it is just to find what it is we are meant to be doing with ourselves. Perhaps these ambitions have played on our minds and have slipped away long ago. Perhaps it has all become too late. Whatever opportunities there were, they now belong to the past, and we are left with the frustration and the grief of what might have been. 'If only' is probably the most debilitating thought that we can have. This was Zachariah.

Luke tells us that Zachariah was 'upright' in the sight of God. He was a well respected pillar of his community and, in spite of all his doubts and misgivings, he continued to carry out his duties faithfully but none of this bought him any closer to what he most wanted. Where did it get him? Zachariah had begun to distrust God and I imagine thoughts raged through his mind:

> Where is God?
> Is God's only concern centred on what I can do for him?
> Does he not care a speck about what I want?
> Why should he?

In his darkness Zachariah may have concluded that his heart's desire was of no interest to God at all. When this happens, grace can go out of our lives, and we become dis-graced. We bleat like sheep, nagging like a scratchy record as others begin to avoid us. We can be like this whether or not we believe in God. Somehow that thing that we want always eludes us. We do our best, tolerate the intolerable and work our socks off but nothing brings us what we most want. Perhaps it's the environment we live in that has got in the way, or perhaps it's the boss, or maybe it's God. Perhaps we are just fated, or perhaps it's that bit of bad luck that always seems to dog us.

So Luke's gospel starts with the angel from God coming to an ordinary, upright, but deeply frustrated person while he was going about his duties. He came with a message to say that Zachariah was going to sire a son who was going to announce the person of Jesus to the world. But it wasn't to be a glorious beginning for Zachariah. In that moment with the angel, when God made himself known to him, Zachariah displayed all the distrust, cynicism and frustration of an unfulfilled man. Luke records that he said 'How can I be sure of this?' (Luke 1:18) in a conversation which might be roughly translated as follows:

> Zachariah. Elizabeth, your wife, will bear you a son!
> Well, well - there you go...
> You will give him the name John.
> Do you really expect me to believe this?
> He will be great in the sight of the Lord.
> Are you sure?
> He will make ready a people for the Lord.
> Yes, and I suppose that pigs might fly!
> (Adapted from Luke 1:13-17)

At this inauspicious point, something rather strange happened to Zachariah. He was struck dumb and couldn't speak. Zachariah's life had been shaken and now it was time to be silent and to reflect on what the angel had told him.

There are times when life-shaking experiences force us to withdraw so that we can hear what God is saying to us. Life-shaking experiences come in different forms. The death of a loved one or the loss of a job through redundancy can cause huge upheaval. In my case it was illness that caused me to look at my life again and to make some hard decisions. My story is not a particularly unusual one. My illness meant that I couldn't go on as I was and that I had to change. God stayed with me and held me 'upright' although I deserved nothing. The unworthiness of my 'uprightness' bought me very low and like Zachariah, I had to withdraw as I accepted what I had gained through my changing life, but also to grieve at what I had lost and left behind. I felt, in my time of silence, that I had a kindred spirit in Zachariah, who went on to write a beautiful song ending with these words:

> ...to shine on those living in darkness
> and in the shadow of death,
> to guide our feet into the path of peace. (Luke 1:79)

It was in his powerless silence that Zachariah got the point, and it was in powerless silence that I had to grasp the same point as well. And it was in powerless silence that this book was born.

Powerless yet searching

Zachariah was in a silent darkness of spirit, yet he had to do something. He distrusted God and was unable to speak, but I think his condition might have been rather worse than just not being able to speak because people had to 'make signs' to him in order to communicate. I lost my voice once for a period of eight months many years ago. For some of that time I couldn't even whisper, but on no occasion did anyone have to make signs to me. Although I couldn't speak, I was able to hear, so I get the impression that Zachariah had lost both powers of speech and hearing. He was committed to silence in every sense of the word.

Recovery for Zachariah came through a heated argument involving Elizabeth, which he could see was happening but could not hear to understand. Because Zachariah was mute, his neighbours were arguing with his wife over what to call the child. Once they finally got Zachariah to understand what they were talking about, he wrote on a tablet 'His name is John,' (Luke 1:63), and at that moment Zachariah put away his distrust of God and came out of his silence.

So Luke's gospel opens with a man who, like my dad, had a problem with God. Yet in spite of that he came to realise that God had made possible something that was impossible. He understood his powerlessness before God but, even with his lack of understanding, God had reached out to him in an impossible way. Elizabeth, his wife, had given him a son even though she was well past the age for bearing children. 'His name is John!' shouted Zachariah in triumph about his son, who was to proclaim Jesus, and with that shout of triumph he realised that at last he had found the desire of his heart.

Zachariah represents a challenge to us. Are we prepared to think that God is reaching out to us as he reached out to Zachariah? We won't find any answer by ourselves because, if we try, we will merely sink back into the oblivion of unanswered questions. We need God to open our understanding, as Zachariah needed God to open his understanding. The process of finding God might cause upheaval but, through it, we will find the desire of our hearts or possibly something even beyond our present horizons.

Someone once said, 'every end is a new beginning'. The next chapter describes journeys that ended with new beginnings. These journeys were undertaken by pairs or groups of people in order to find Jesus - God in the world. Each journey was a painful one in its way, but each journey resulted in Jesus being found. Look at these journeys in the next chapter, and look at the searchers. The stories may be familiar, but I believe if we look at them again we will see new things to speak to our circumstances.

CHAPTER 2

FINDING JESUS IN DARKNESS

Your father and I have been anxiously searching for you
(Luke 2:48)

Jesus was born in darkness and he died in darkness. He came into our world that was, and still is, filled with darkness. This is the theme taken up at the beginning of John's gospel, where Jesus is described as the light shining in the darkness. (John 1:5)

Chapter two of Luke's gospel is about people in twos or threes or in groups all looking for Jesus. They found him in very different ways. One of these journeys to Jesus was rough, another spectacularly and delightfully quick, a third was tortuous and another meant a long, long wait. The last one was where the searchers had lost Jesus and were trying to find him again. One or more of these journeys might reflect something of our own experience.

Mary and Joseph – the journey to Bethlehem

The journey to Bethlehem was very rough. It involved a walk of over 100 km from Nazareth to Bethlehem. We like to have a cosy feeling over the Christmas story but I think that cosiness was far from what Mary and Joseph experienced,. This journey was the darkest time of their young lives. Firstly, Mary was in an advanced stage of an illegitimate pregnancy, bearing the threatened stigma of immorality. Secondly, to make it worse, the journey was all about some census ordered by a foreign power in occupation of their homeland and therefore held no useful purpose for them. It was a miserable, despairing journey that they undertook to find Jesus.

But this couple, Mary and Joseph, were exceptional. What other woman was there who could be the mother of God in this world? What other person would have accepted the news of her on-coming pregnancy with so much grace? We might want to reverence Mary but

19

she held no answers for the questions we may have. Only the baby she carried had the answers, but Luke records twice that she 'treasured up all these things and pondered them in her heart' (Luke 2:19,51)

And then there was Joseph. How I wish we gave more recognition to this extraordinary man. How many men would have shown such obedience to God and so much love to both God and to his intended wife? The story of Joseph is related in the first chapter of Matthew's gospel in verses 18-24, and it is not difficult to imagine the torment that he went through. A man like Joseph was needed at Jesus' birth, just as another Joseph, of equal strength, was needed at his death.

Their journey will speak to anyone who has walked a rough road in life, anyone who seems to have had more than their fair share of knocks yet hangs on to their faith. In my working life I knew a man who worked for a large international company who was a Christian. For as long as I had known him he had suffered from leukaemia. After I was diagnosed with my own form of cancer, he would always be sure to ask me how things were before we got down to business. Indeed, he was one of my strengths during that difficult time. More recently I learned that his wife had also been diagnosed with cancer; yet nothing changed. Always we started our business on how I was coping. Mary and Joseph are honoured very highly in the Christian church and I too honour my friend highly.

The shepherds

We know nothing about these shepherds, but their search for Jesus was a short one. They were about their routine job in fields near the town of Bethlehem when they received an unexpected visit from an angel followed by a whole company of angels. So how many is that? A company, by old military definition, might be anywhere between 75 and 200 men, so I think that Luke is leading us to conclude that the field became fairly crowded!

> *Glory to God in the highest heaven,*
> *and on earth peace to those on whom his favour rests."*
> *(Luke 2:14)*

These shepherds were not easily frightened. They lived their lives in the open, ready to face whatever threatened the sheep, but this was something else. So the angel called to them:

> ...do not be afraid...you will find a baby wrapped in cloths and lying in a manger (Luke 2:10-12)

At this point the shepherds were faced with a choice. They could either stay where they were, or go and find him. There was no hesitation. They grabbed the opportunity given to them, and went.

This speaks of men and women who are suddenly confronted by God. They become aware of a need within themselves, and are drawn to something without fully understanding what it is they are looking for. Crashing into their consciousness is the realisation that God, the creator, is reaching out to them. For them, finding Jesus is but a short journey of acceptance. But anybody having this experience faces a problem - whether it is really God reaching out, or whether it stems from some form of emotional imagination. The answer to this dilemma comes in the decision that the shepherds made.

> Let's go to Bethlehem and see this thing that has happened, which the Lord has told us about. So they hurried off... (Luke 2:15-16)

The important word here is 'they'. In my experience, when God speaks, he seems always to speak to more than one person. So if we experience God reaching out to us, we will probably find that he has also reached out to others around us. God does not leave us on our own.

I did not find Jesus in this way, but the presence of God has come crashing into my life on a number of occasions since. Like most, I go through times of terrible doubt and then, unexpectedly, a great shaft of light opens up my understanding. When this happens, it is an exciting, exhilarating and deeply memorable experience, and one that I have always shared with others. For sure the shepherds never forgot that night.

The wise men

Occasionally throughout this book, I will refer to other gospel accounts in order to enrich our understanding of Luke's account. One reason that

I have included the story of the wise men, to be found in Matthew 2:1-12, is because it is so well known by most people, whether or not they come to church or call themselves Christians. However, the main reason that I want to include it is because the wise men's experience of finding Jesus was very different from the experience shared by the shepherds. Their journey was more of a long, tortuous search. What both wise men and shepherds hold in common is that we see both find Jesus in darkness.

These men had discerned a star which revealed to them that something extra-ordinary that was about to happen. The 'King of the Jews' was about to be born and he was someone worthy of their worship. Beyond that, they knew little as they travelled from the east. They were looking for a king, so what better place to look than in Jerusalem, the capital city. Coming from afar, they innocently walked into the clutches of Herod the Great, a tyrant who would ruthlessly exterminate any challenge to his rule. So asking 'where is the one who has been born king of the Jews?' (Matt 2:2) was not, in the circumstances, the wisest question to ask.

It is a miracle therefore that these men emerged out of the darkness of Jerusalem to continue their journey. It was only then that the star that they had seen re-appeared in the night sky to guide them those few short miles from Jerusalem to Bethlehem, where they found Jesus and laid their gifts before him.

I am so fascinated by this story because it speaks volumes about my own search for Jesus. At a very young age I was aware of something – what, I don't know. As I grew older I knew that I had to find answers. My search led me, blundering at times, into the wrong places, sometimes saying all the wrong things. Looking back, I am amazed that I found Jesus - but God mercifully reached out and found me. Once found I was able to lay out before Jesus whatever gifts or talents I had been given. So the story of the wise men is for anyone who, like me, struggles on a tortuous path.

Would you believe it?
You the struggling
With hearts that are longing
Evermore seeking
For the way that is right

Would you believe it?
You the despairing
With hearts that are darkening
By forces threatening
Held in the night

Would you believe it?
Someone is reigning
For hearts that are opening
While he is shepherding
us to the light.

Would you believe it?
For he is nearing
Your heart that is lighting
Seeking and finding
Your lifelong delight

Would you believe it?
This God is needing
Your heart that is treasuring
The gift of believing
in this God of Might

Simeon and Anna

After the birth, Mary and Joseph took the baby to the Temple in Jerusalem as an act of purification, in accordance with the Law of Moses. Serving at the Temple were Simeon and Anna. Both were now elderly but both had waited, confident that they would see whom God would send. They waited and they prayed constantly - until one day, as they were going about their daily routines in the Temple, they saw the baby. Both knew immediately that their waiting search was over. God had given a light for revelation to the Gentiles and the glory of his people Israel (Luke 2:32).

These two represent all those people who serve responsibly and endlessly in our churches year after year. They are people who are often unremembered by those around them but who are never forgotten by

God. Simeon and Anna represent those who quietly and unceremoniously pray constantly - for the world, the nation, and the church, and whose prayers are responsible for bringing about God's grace in a way that most of us know little about.

Searching for Jesus continues throughout life. We search for him and find him and then search again and find him again - as the final story in this chapter shows.

Mary and Joseph – the journey to Jerusalem

It was now twelve years later, and the child grew and became strong; he was filled with wisdom and the grace of God was with him. (Luke 2:40) You can almost see the fireworks about to come! They did come - on another journey that Mary and Joseph took to Jerusalem. But this time Jesus went too.

For Mary and Joseph, this journey did not hold the misery and despair of their previous trip. This journey was a happy occasion, like a holiday - off to Jerusalem to celebrate the Passover with family and friends, quite unlike that nightmare twelve years earlier. On that journey to Bethlehem they found Jesus, but on this journey to Jerusalem they lost him. We might speculate over how this came about, but I hardly think this matters a great deal. The fact is that Jesus wasn't where they thought he would be. So after a day's journey, when darkness was falling, they hurried back to Jerusalem. One can only imagine the agony of the three days it took to find him. They searched everywhere - where they stayed, all the people that they visited, pleaded with the authorities but, as darkness fell each night – he was nowhere to be found. Then on the third day:

> Have you tried the temple?
> What would he be doing in the temple?
> Well, he was fascinated by it when he was there.
> Yes, that's because we took him there.
> Listen - try the temple!
> He wouldn't go there on his own, would he?
> I don't know.
> Not amongst all those important people...
> Try it, you've nothing to lose.

And of course, that is where he was - in the temple among the teachers, listening to them and asking questions. We have been anxiously searching for you (Luke 2:48), cried a relieved mother and step-father, as they hugged him to themselves again.

Christians, who have made a real commitment to serving God, might some day suddenly find that somehow Jesus doesn't seem to be there anymore. It is as if we try to put him in a box. 'That's where you are, Jesus. That is your place and I can manage perfectly well with you there.' The trouble is that Jesus will shred any kind of box that we try to put him in, just as burst out of the tomb on Easter Day.

I recall giving a talk many years ago to my church as a very young man. Although I hadn't been preaching very long, the thought came to me on a commuter train speeding to London one morning that I was to tell my church, based on this story, that they had lost Jesus. I was aghast! I remonstrated with God - 'I can't tell them that!' But the thought was insistent and, after talking it over with others, my doubts were overcome. The church was devastated but they were spiritually awake enough to realise the truth in what was said.

Do we identify with one of these journeys? Maybe we have experienced more than one type of journey in our life, but still our understanding remains in darkness. Or maybe we have stopped searching for any answers at all. Maybe we are at a point in our lives where we are being taken out of our comfort-zone towards something that we have never done before. The message from the angels is the same for us today. Don't be afraid! (Luke 2:10) Remember it was always two or more people travelling together, so there are always others who will help us along the way.

One thing that comes out of these stories is that finding Jesus is for anyone. It is for the young and the old. It is for the gifted and those still seeking their gifts. It is for the rich and the poor. It is for those whose lives are humdrum and those whose lives are in turmoil. It is for everyone, no matter what their race or their beliefs or their colour. But for now, the baby who had come to reconcile all to God was known by only a diverse few. It would remain that way until a man, appointed by God, would declare him to a world that was desperately in need of him. That man was John the Baptist.

CHAPTER 3

JOHN THE BAPTIST

I tell you, among those born of women there is no one greater than John...
(Luke 7:28)

About eighteen years have now passed, and Jesus has grown to a man about thirty years old. At his birth only a very few people knew there was something extraordinary about him but now most of those people, other than his mother, would have died. We hear no more of Joseph, the shepherds or the wise men. We hear no more of Zachariah, Elizabeth, Simeon and Anna who were all elderly when Jesus was born. But there was one person left still to mark his 'birth' and, although he was the last person recorded to recognise Jesus in his obscurity, he was hardly the least.

This was John the Baptist, son of old Zachariah.

No one greater.

> In the fifteenth year of the reign of Tiberius Caesar
> something extraordinary happened!
> When Pontius Pilate was governor of Judea
> the word came to John, son of Zachariah, in the desert
> When Herod was Tetrarch of Galilee
> John went into the country around Jordan preaching a baptism of
> repentance for the forgiveness of sins.
> (Adapted from Luke 3:1-3)

John the Baptist lived in the desert, wore camel's hair, and ate wild honey. He preached that all people were sinners and, as sinners, they fell into two categories. In the first category were those who accepted that they were sinners and repented their sin. In the second category were those who did not accept that they were sinners. Instead they justified themselves because they were descended from Father Abraham. Those in the second category he called a brood of vipers. He didn't mince his words!

Supposing John were preaching repentance and forgiveness of sins today in the wilderness of London, Birmingham or Manchester. He would still divide us into two categories. Some would accept that we are sinners while others would attempt to excuse their sin. 'After all, God is a God of love, isn't he. I've done my best and you can't ask for more than that, now can you?' Many would nod agreement to this creed – but not John. Those who attempted to excuse their sin were branded a brood of vipers. He preached that their talk was both poisonous and wrong.

Jesus said of John '...among those born of women there is no one greater than John,' (Luke 7:28). I have puzzled over this. No one greater? That seems difficult to comprehend even taking account of Jesus' own national history. Is this passionate man who preached in the desert and died an early death greater than Abraham, the father of nations? Is he greater than Moses, who led the Israelites out of Egypt and through the Red Sea? Is he greater than the prophet Elijah, who brought down fire from heaven at Mount Carmel? Can it be that he is greater than David who killed the giant Goliath and later became king – and the list goes on.

Jesus said there was no one greater than John because, through the Holy Spirit of God, he recognised exactly who Jesus was and, at the time, no one else (probably not even his mother) wholly recognised that. He realised not only that Jesus was God in this world but he also clearly saw who he was by comparison. He told the crowds:

> ...one who is more powerful than I will come, the thongs of whose sandals I am not worthy to untie. (Luke 3:16)

Untying his sandals

Actually John and my dad shared the same problem about God. He realised only too clearly that, as my dad had realised, there was a vast difference between himself and God - so vast as to be unfathomable. He knew that Jesus was in the world and that Jesus was God and he, John, was a mere man. One was the creator of the universe and the other was a mere speck.

Then came the day when John's life was overturned. It was the day when his problem was put to the test. On that day, Jesus appeared amongst the crowd in the desert. This was the day when John was confronted by God in the world, 'the thongs on whose sandals, I'm not worthy to untie.' But Jesus had not come to take over, but had come to be baptised along with everybody else. For John, that was quite impossible. Luke simply records that 'Jesus was baptised too' (Luke 3:21) but John's mind must have been in turmoil. Jesus had come to him...to him...no that can't be right! We might imagine the conversation adapted from Matthew 3:13-15 where John is vainly trying to deter Jesus.

> Jesus, what are you doing here?
> You know why I have come
> But I'm baptising people
> So then baptise me with them
> I can't do that
> Why not?
> Because it's you that has to baptise me
> Let it be this way for now, OK?
> I don't understand but if you say so, let it be for now.

To understand John's difficulty we might imagine that I am on a large sandy beach, where I pick up a single tiny grain of sand and put it into a small glass jar. Even though the glass jar is small, it dwarfs the tiny speck of sand that it contains. Then I put the glass jar into my pocket with the speck of sand within and drive up to Manchester where I am going to see my son, his wife and my two small grandchildren. When I arrive I tell them that I think that they should have the children baptised. Then I confuse them utterly by producing my little glass jar with the speck of sand within it and tell them that I think that it would be a good idea that the baptism of their children should be carried out by this speck of sand. They would, of course, know by then that I had taken complete leave of my senses!

This is something of what John must have thought when Jesus came to him for baptism in the Jordan desert. John's understanding was probably clearer than anybody's. This was God, creator of the universe coming to a speck for baptism. How could this be? But it was alright for John, the speck, to baptise the creator of the universe, because this was the way that God wished it to be. 'You are my Son, whom I love; with you I am well pleased,' (Luke 3:22) said a voice from heaven as Jesus was being baptised.

What was John saying out there in the desert? What was he telling all who came to him in the desert of their lives? He came with a message from God about sin; but he also came with a message of hope.

John's message of sin

Luke tells us that John 'went into all the country around the Jordan, preaching a baptism of repentance for the forgiveness of sins' (Luke 3:3). His message was stark. Yes, we might have a problem with God, with understanding God, or even with accepting God; but John was at pains to point something else out as well.

God has a problem with us too – and that problem is sin.

The word 'sin' is probably the most misunderstood word in the English language. To some it denotes religious condemnation, but to most it means some form of sexual deviation or immorality. Sin does include sexual immorality, but it has a much deeper meaning. Sin represents everything that separates us from God. Sin encompasses all the problems that we have with God, and also encompasses all the problems that God has with us.

John had a simple message about sin for those who came to him in the desert. He told them not to be greedy. He told them to share clothes and food, he told them not to sponge off others and he told them to stop their culture of blame (Luke 3:10-14). But greed only displays the tip of the iceberg, and it leads into all manner of other things. Greed often induces jealousy over what others have, which in turn spirals into a sense of failure and purposelessness. Greed can create abuse along with rage and hatred, and yes, sexual immorality as well.

The message from John comes to our own desert. Greed is in all of us, one way or another. Greed is imbued in our society as we lurch from one crisis to another. Greed is behind every economic recession; every redundancy; and every repossession. We turn to our politicians to straighten things out; but to our disappointment, and to theirs as well, we find they can't straighten things out, no matter how hard they try.

Hence, I believe that God has a problem with us, and it follows that God doesn't like the way we are any more than we like the way we have become. So the gap between God and us is not one sided. It comes from both sides. Not only do we have a problem accepting God but he has a problem accepting what we are. This is sin. Sin is all this mixed together and produces a huge gap that separates God from us. We might display this graphically through a simple illustration.

John's message of hope

But John also came to a desert, to those oppressed by the Romans and the Jewish leaders, who flocked to him and heard a message of hope. He also brings that message of hope to those who are oppressed today. Life for many has become a desert of economic depression. The work-place has become an uphill struggle. Financial hardship, whether threatened or actual, affects both health and marriage. John's message of hope is that

> *Every valley shall be filled in,*
> *every mountain and hill made low.*
> *The crooked roads shall become straight,*
> *the rough ways smooth (Luke 3:5)*

He proclaimed that God himself was coming into the world to help us through rough times. He would be someone alongside us in our uphill struggles and through our periods of depression. John announced the person of Jesus who, through his death on the cross, would bridge the gap that separates God from us. But Luke has a question to ask before we leave chapter three. How do we know that Jesus can do this? How do we know that what Jesus says is true? Does Jesus – does anyone – have the authority to reconcile us to the vast creator God?

Credentials

When I was faced with having a tricky operation, I was quite understandably concerned about the skill of the surgeon who proposed the surgery. So I asked him for his credentials. What was the depth of his experience? How many times had he performed this operation? Could I trust this man with my body and with my life? However, when it came down to it, my acceptance of this doctor amounted to an exercise in faith. It is the same when faced with the person of Jesus. What are his credentials? Is he all that he's cracked up to be? Can he really make possible a relationship between us and the creator-god? Can we really find life after death through him?

Acceptance of Jesus will always come down to a matter of faith. Nevertheless Luke, being a doctor himself, knew the importance of credentials and therefore he would perfectly understand if we were to ask for references. So imagine that three letters come through our post.

We open the first one and read:

> To those reading this book. Jesus described me as the greatest to be born of woman but I must tell you that, even if I am the greatest, I am not worthy to untie the thongs of his sandals. I baptised him in the river because he told me to but you must be baptised in the name of Jesus. Get ready for him and your mountains will be lowered and your pitfalls filled.
>
> Yours ever.
> John (the Baptist)

Then we open the second letter, which reads:

> My children, Jesus is my beloved son in whom I love and am well pleased. Listen to him.
>
> Yours forever.
> God

And finally we open the third letter:

> Dear reader, be confident that Jesus is God in the world. I have traced his human roots back to God. You can follow it in my third chapter but keep on reading the gospel.
>
> Faithfully yours,
> Luke

John was now reaching the end of his ministry, and the end of his life in the world. John wasn't afraid of anybody. He didn't distinguish the rich from the poor, so when Herod the tetrarch (not Herod the Great from chapter two) decided, out of curiosity, to take a day trip to see what was going on, he found himself at the receiving end of a public ear-bashing over his adultery. This must have bought a few sniggers from those within earshot but it didn't amuse Herod. John was flung into prison.

By contrast, Jesus was baptised and his ministry about to start. But he didn't start in the way that we might have expected.

CHAPTER FOUR

WILDERNESS

He has sent me to proclaim freedom for the prisoners...
(Luke 4:18)

Nothing separated Jesus from God. No sin came between them. Jesus had no problems with the vastness of God, because he came from God and was God. Equally, God had no problems with Jesus because there was nothing about Jesus that was impure. 'This is my Son whom I love,' said God from a cloud at Jesus' baptism (see chapter three), 'with you (Jesus) I am well pleased'. God and Jesus were totally in tune with each other:

GOD——JESUS

So I've found it a bit confusing that Jesus then had to go from his baptism into the wilderness for a long period. Surely he was now ready to start his ministry? In the wilderness he starved himself for forty days and nights and then met with the devil who tried everything he could to put something between him and God. Weakened though he was, Jesus resisted all the temptations, and the devil left him.

But what did Jesus achieve from this difficult time? Actually, he left one wilderness and went into another. He had left John the Baptist, whose voice still cried in the desert, and now it was time for Jesus to confront his own wilderness and, with it, the problems and sins that ensnare all of us and which result in our separation from God.

Wilderness starts with a question: 'what do we want?' Wilderness is absent while we have the answer, but is evident while we struggle with the question. However we should accept that wilderness periods are very necessary as we sort ourselves out. Nevertheless I have met some who have been in a wilderness all the time that I have known them. Prolonged periods of wilderness can result when we cling to a wrong decision or a wrong idea, particularly when it concerns something fundamental about ourselves.

In Luke chapter four, Jesus confronts his demons through three temptations concerning wealth, power and freedom. These things are not bad in themselves, but craving for them could lead us to get stuck in some form of wilderness. Jesus had to experience this for himself. The stakes were high for Jesus, because if he didn't deal with these temptations, then his mission would fail before it had even started.

What do we most want? Wealth

> *He ate nothing during those days, and at the end of them he was hungry. The devil said to him 'If you are the Son of God, tell this stone to become bread.' (Luke 4:2-3)*

What if someone came up and asked us what we most want? Most of us would answer something like, 'I want to have millions of pounds. Perhaps win the lottery so that I could have everything. Big house, no work, endless holiday'....and so on. Is there anything the matter with wanting these things? Are we wrong to desire wealth? I would be lying through my teeth if I told you that I scorned wealth. No, I would like to have lots of money like most others. Furthermore, I have met some very happy people who are wealthy, and I have also met many wealthy people who are clearly far from happy. But the people who are most tragic are those who yearn after wealth, ever climbing mountains in search of more wealth, but never finding enough. So they cling to the idea that wealth is the key to happiness, which in turn leads them into a wilderness of possessions and results in separation from God. Again, we might understand this graphically using the same illustration found in chapter three.

GOD—|WEAL⊤H|—US

'People do not live on bread alone,' (Luke 4:4), is Jesus' classic reply to this temptation. Jesus knew the importance of wealth but also knew that it was not the most important matter of life. If wealth comes and we are content with it, then that is a wonderful blessing; and God does bless some of his children this way. But a craving for wealth which is never satisfied separates us from God and it is only when we realise that there are other things more important than wealth that we can we emerge from this wilderness.

What do we most want? Power

> *The devil led him to Jerusalem and had him stand on the highest*
> *point of the temple. 'If you are the Son of God,' he said, 'throw*
> *yourself down from here. For it is written:*
>   *"He will command his angels concerning you*
>   *to guard you carefully;*
>   *they will lift you up in their hands,*
>   *so that you will not strike your foot against a stone"'*
> *(Luke 4:9-11)*

I have taken this temptation next because, for me, it follows hard on the first. To the question 'what do we most want?', a good percentage would reply, 'I want to be successful. I want to be the best. I don't want to fail in anything. I don't do failure'. Some would have difficulty in deciding between wealth and power because, in many people's minds, they go hand-in-glove.

Again, I have met contented people in positions of power and others who contentedly have no desire for any position of power at all. The most tragic are those who yearn for power and never have enough. Years ago I was inwardly moved by a talk given by Chuck Colson at St Helens Bishopsgate in London. He was one of President Nixon's advisors, and was heavily involved in the Watergate scandal of the 1970s. I will always remember him saying that his ambition for power led him to crave promotion, but that every step-up only created more craving for the next step-up. He was never satisfied. The yearning for power corrupted him. It corrupted the Nixon government, as it corrupts governments and businesses today. Those who yearn for power find themselves in a wilderness, separated from God.

GOD —|POWER|— US

Jesus said in reply, 'do not put the Lord your God to the test' (Luke 4:12). For some, a position of power is their destiny and we should pray for them because they can often find themselves in lonely places and constantly being put to the test.

What do we most want? Freedom

> *The devil led (Jesus) up to a high place and showed him in an instant all the kingdoms of the world. And he said to him 'I will give you all their authority and splendour; it has been given to me and I can give it to anyone I want to. If you worship me, it will all be yours'*
> *(Luke 4:5-7)*

The 'promise' of authority and splendour (power and wealth) is taken a step further and becomes the saddest of the three temptations. 'I must have. Life is all about me and is all about what I want. I will do anything and will stop at nothing in order to get everything I want.'

The paradox is that this, which is the most 'in your face' of the three temptations, is also the most subtle and destructive. 'Must haves' think that to be free is to have what they want, but in truth, falling for this temptation only produces a downward spiral that follows this type of pattern:

We must have
It is our right to have
Someone else is to blame if we don't have.
And so we become increasingly dependent on someone else
and freedom is lost

Perhaps we struggle to understand what is meant by freedom. Books have been written on the subject by philosophical minds far more intelligent than mine, but I liked how a Russian guide defined it to me recently. 'Freedom,' she said simply, 'is taking responsibility'. If we accept this small beginning of understanding, then we might discern that sadly we live in a culture where the opposite is true. Far from taking responsibility, we have become increasingly dependent on politicians, doctors, teachers or social workers (to name but a few), all of whom are to blame if they don't give us what we 'must have'. We might not think of ourselves as 'must haves' but our society is so imbued with this culture that it imprisons us in some way. Loss of our inner freedom separates us from God, who desires our freedom above all things. (Anyone doubting that God wants this for us might look at John 8:36 and then Galatians 5:1).

GOD ─┤IMPRISONMENT├─ US

Jesus replied, 'worship the Lord your God and serve him only' (Luke 4:8). We need freedom to worship, freedom to love, freedom from poverty in mind and spirit, freedom to say what we honestly believe and, above all, freedom to take responsibility. In other words we are not to be dependent on anyone other than God.

Jesus was dependent on God, and so nothing separated him from God. As he prepared to leave the wilderness, he knew that he needed to be rock solid with God because he was to begin his ministry, where he would meet many challenging situations. His first challenge came from somewhere unexpected. It came from his hometown – Nazareth.

Nazareth

Jesus' ministry started in pain and finished in pain. One of the first things that Jesus did when he came away from the wilderness was to go home. So he went to Nazareth, and into his church as he had always done. Only this time was not like any other time. In church, he read to the congregation:

> 'The Spirit of the Lord is on me,
> because he has anointed me
> to proclaim good news to the poor.
> He has sent me to proclaim freedom for the prisoners
> and recovery of sight for the blind,
> to set the oppressed free,
> to proclaim the year of the Lord's favour.' (Luke 4:18)

The passage that he was reading is from Isaiah in the Old Testament. It represented all that he had come to understand in the wilderness - that it would be through him that men and women could find the freedom that would fulfil their lives. It would be through him that they would no longer be separated from God. The congregation were incredulous:

Isn't this Joseph's son?
Saying these things? Well now!
He's a carpenter, isn't he?
Who does he think he is?
Anybody would think he's God Almighty!
I think he's got a bit above himself, don't you?
Yes, my Harold says he's going to have a word with the vicar about him.

He lives here, they thought.
He's ours, they thought.
We own him, they thought.
We can control him.
He is our possession.

The home church thought that they could control Jesus, just as a man wants to possess and control his wealth. But Jesus was not some object to be possessed. So he attacked their complacency, and their assumption that they were God's chosen. Their reaction against him was violent. They drove him out of the town, then tried to kill him. They were so beside themselves with rage that they were intent on killing Mary's son – intent on killing the son of their neighbour. Such was the terrible wilderness that they were in.

As they dragged him toward a cliff to hurl him off, we read that 'he walked right through the crowd and went on his way' (Luke 4:30). This was Jesus, free to be himself and to say what needed to be said; but freedom for Jesus came at a price, and that price was very high. He was walking away from the place he grew up, away from the love of his mother and brothers. From now on, they would only be able to visit him away from home. This was the price that he paid for refusing to be owned by anybody other than God. It is the price we might also have to pay if we are to gain the freedom we most earnestly desire. The pain of gaining freedom can be huge.

Capernaum

He went to another town in Galilee, called Capernaum. Once again he went into the church and taught there. While there he was confronted by someone 'possessed of a demon' and Jesus commanded the demon to leave him.

There are many demons rampaging around our country today. Many people, particularly young people, have lost their freedom to twenty first century demons such as:

The conformity-demon – having to be like everyone else
The addiction-demon – anything to forget our inadequacies
The diet-demon – hooked on fashion

It's distressing to see people imprisoned by these things. It is like any other wilderness that separates us from God. Jesus came to proclaim freedom for the prisoners, to give us freedom just to be ourselves and to be responsible for ourselves and for those around us. Is that too much to ask of God? The answer is 'no,' because that is exactly what God wants for us.

Simon's mother-in-law

In Capernaum lived a man called Simon who, we will find, features heavily in Luke's gospel. He had invited Jesus home for supper, but unfortunately the cook – Simon's mother-in-law – was sick, with a high fever. We are told that Jesus rebuked the fever and it left her, so she could get on with what she was good at doing. Cooking the supper! This is the first of Jesus' miracles that Luke recorded.

What does this mean to any who are sick? Maybe we have prayed earnestly for the sickness to leave us but nothing has happened, at least not like it happened for Simon's mother-in-law when Jesus came to visit. Sickness can be frightening, and we can become debilitated by the fear of where it might lead us - to doctors, to hospital, to uncomfortable treatments, to death. If we become possessed by these things, we might become paralysed and lose the ability to function. Effectively, we might lose our freedom.

My illness frightened me and I became possessed by fear. For a time I was unable to continue functioning in my ministry, and my work deteriorated. I have had to learn to come to terms with the condition so that it does not possess me. From this I learned that those who are sick may or may not be cured but I also learned of a greater need. I needed to be free of possession by sickness, because Jesus came to release the oppressed.

Solitude

At the end of a busy day, Jesus went off to a quiet place. He started the chapter in the wilderness and finished it in solitude. No-one disturbed him in the obscurity of his wilderness, but here in the solitude of evening, many people came to him, pleading with him to stay. But Jesus was free and close to God. He was free to go elsewhere, and that is what he chose to do. This is the freedom we yearn for, consciously or unconsciously. Not hide-bound by tradition or expectation; not shackled to a desk or to the bottle; not chained by diet or by illness. Instead, free to be ourselves and to do what God created us to do.

Jesus was free. The time of his birth was over and his ministry in Galilee had begun.

Part Two: Galilee

CHAPTER FIVE

CHANGE

Forget the former things;
do not dwell on the past.
See, I am doing a new thing!
(Isaiah 43:18-19)

God delights in new things. He doesn't stay still, and this can be infuriating at times. He pushes us gently and sometimes not so gently on to new horizons and new challenges. Yet God knows that we need time to adjust to the idea of change. Wilderness is a time when we need to consider and ponder, to rest while we weigh up with possible uncertainty the new thing that God seems to wants us to do. Times of wilderness are very necessary for all of us.

However, when we get stuck in the wilderness, it is as if we have gone to sleep and not woken up. We have found our comfort zone and have become 'bedridden', unable and unwilling to get up and undertake anything new. Old and not so old can get stuck in their ways, resisting change, hanging grimly to former things, constantly dwelling on the past. Times of wilderness are necessary, but when we get stuck in the wilderness we become separated from God.

Old and new clothes

Jesus brings this out with a story at the end of Luke chapter five, which sums up what the chapter is all about. The story is about clothes and it goes something like this:

'Want to hear a story?'
    'OK'
'There's this woman, right?'
    'Woman?'
'Well, it could have been a man.'
    'Make up your mind!'
'Well that's it'
    'She couldn't make up her mind'
'about what to wear'
    'Every morning'
'She'd go to her wardrobe'
    'and look'
'and look'
    'and then choose the same dress'
'because she wouldn't dare'
    'wear anything new'
'That dress must have got smelly'
    'It certainly got old'
'Then one morning'
    'She took out the same old dress and'
'Horror and devastation...'
    'A hole'
'In the dress'
    'So she put it on'
'Hole and all'

'and legged it'
'to Marks and Spencer'
'to buy a new dress'
'very sensible'
'or so you would think'
'but think again'
'When she got home'
'she went to the kitchen'
'got out some scissors'
'and cut out a patch'
'from the new dress'
'and then sewed the patch'
'from the new dress'
'onto the old one'
'The new dress was ruined'
'and the old one'
'looked ridiculous'
'and so did she.'

This chapter of Luke's gospel is about change. It is about the difficulty of accepting change, and the devastation that change can create in our lives.

Simon, the leper and Levi

Jesus was in Galilee. He went to broken people, sick people, worried people, guilty people, despairing people – these people became his earthly companions. However, Jesus had no intention of patching up their problems and letting them continue the way they were. The solution had to be far more fundamental than any sticking plaster ever could be. The story of the old and new garments gives a clear message that the old had to be replaced with something new. Patching over problems was not the answer.

There are three people in this chapter whose lives were about to change from the roots up. These three were very different from each other. Firstly there was Simon the fisherman on Lake Genneseret - Jesus healed his mother-in-law in chapter four. Secondly there was a leper with sores all over him, and thirdly there was Levi, who was a tax collector.

Simon Peter

'Go away from me,' said Simon on his knees before Jesus, 'Lord, I am a sinful man' (Luke 5:8). He had been listening to Jesus all day, because it was easy to listen to Jesus all day. Jesus even borrowed Simon's boat to speak from. That made Simon feel just a bit important – a head above all the others in the teeming crowd that was listening to Jesus. It made up a bit for the failure that happened last night. In spite of fishing all night, they had caught absolutely nothing. No fish, therefore no money. No money, therefore no food. 'Oh well,' he thought, 'I'll have to go out again soon but not now. I know this lake – bought up on it - man and boy. Leave it for a few days and the fish will be back. Bad though.'

When Jesus eventually finished speaking, he realised that the crowd would not disperse, so he asked Simon to put out into the lake. 'Ah,' thought Simon 'he might be a brilliant speaker. But this is where I belong. This is where I am good - out here on the water. I'll show him how good I am,'

Simon.
Yes, Jesus?
Let down your nets. Do some fishing.
Yes, but...
What's the problem?
No fish, Jesus.
What do you mean – no fish?
What I mean. No fish. Fished all night. Nothing.
Let down your nets, Simon.
But...OK if you insist, but we're wasting time and effort trying...'
(Adapted from Luke 5:4-5)

Famous last words! The nets became so full of fish that they began to break. So they signalled to another boat for help, but there were so many fish that the boat couldn't cope and they were in danger of sinking.

At that moment, Simon saw Jesus with different eyes. This Jesus, this Lord, was way above his league in all respects. He saw Jesus through the same eyes that John the Baptist had in the desert. He saw that beside Jesus, he was a person who was old and worn out, with holes all over, nothing more than a speck by comparison. 'Go away from me, for I am a sinful man,' he said on his knees. At that moment the old Simon was no more. He was free of old Simon and a new Simon had been born. A new Simon. Simon Peter.

The leper

'Lord, if you are willing, you can make me clean,' (Luke 5:12) he said, with his face to the ground in front of Jesus. He lived the life of an outcast but braved the hatred and the taunts of the crowd as they pelted him with whatever came to hand while he made his way steadfastly toward the only person who could help him. Then, begging face down, pathetically trying to hide his hideousness, he said 'Lord, if you are willing...' and he heard the words of Jesus' reply: 'I am willing.' (Luke 5:13)

A man covered in leprosy, rather like an old coat riddled with holes. 'Lord if you will...' he pleaded, and, with that, he became new, free from the disease that had devastated his life. His journey to acceptance was about to begin, as people came to terms with the fact that he was no longer a leper. It would take time but, for the moment, he was new and he knew it.

Levi

'Follow me,' said Jesus to Levi (Luke 5:27). That's all – just 'follow me'. Levi was a tax collector, reviled by people, fed up with his job, and his only friends were tax collectors just like himself. He had heard of Jesus but hadn't taken a great deal of notice - mainly because he didn't think that Jesus would take much notice of him, other than reviling him like all the rest. And then, 'follow me'. So he took off his tax-collecting coat and followed Jesus. With this he was a new man, with a new purpose and a new life, free from the job he hated. He walked away from his old life and into a new one, where he would write a gospel about Jesus under the name of Matthew.

We might think that everybody would be delighted to see the change in these three men; but I wouldn't be so sure. Simon Peter left fishing to follow Jesus, and some may have felt let down by his decision. The leper would take years before he could convince some people that he was no longer a leper and, to some, Levi would remain a tax collector in their memory forever. Simon Peter, the leper and Levi might have changed but they would have found that some around them resisted and even resented the change that had happened within them.

Old and new wine skins

Jesus told another story at the end of chapter five alongside the one about clothes. This story is slightly less easy to understand because it is about old and new wineskins, and we don't have wineskins in the 21st century. However, the theme of the story is very similar. Jesus told his followers not to put new wine into old wine skins. If you do, the old skin will burst and they would lose both skin and wine. The story finishes with Jesus saying:

> ...new wine must be poured into new wineskins. And none of you, after drinking old wine, wants the new, for you say, 'The old is better.' (Luke 5:39)

There is an uncomfortable and rather dark lesson here. This story tells us that the old prefer to stay with the old because they consider the old to be better. We mustn't be surprised when those who are resistant to change clash with those who are seeking something new. Nowhere is this better illustrated than in the story midway through the chapter – the story of five men and a roof.

Five men and a roof

There were five men and one of them was sick. The story about how four of the men got their sick friend to Jesus is generally well known but it wasn't until recently that I realised that this is one of the most hilarious stories in the Bible. But to see the funny side, you have use your imagination.

These men were young - of that I have no doubt. The sick man was paralysed, but his four friends were single-minded in a way that only the young can be. Their reasoning was pure simplicity:

Friend is sick
Jesus can heal friend
Take friend to Jesus.

They were steadfast in their purpose, and innovative with their ideas on how to achieve it. In their young minds it was straightforward, very simple, and they had it worked out - except it didn't turn out quite as they expected because when they arrived at the house where Jesus was, it was so full of people that they couldn't get in. It would have been hard enough for one person to squeeze through but for five of them, including one on a mat, it was impossible.

Undeterred and, perhaps typically for young people, without giving any thought to the consequences of their actions, the four climbed onto the roof, determined to get their friend through that way. Now it is here that I have had to seek some advice about how this roof was constructed. What I am told is that it was flat, and covered with a structure of reeds and branches. Mark's gospel says that they 'dug through the roof'. Luke's gospel has something more substantial in the construction indicating that they lowered the mat 'through the tiles.'

I am sure of one thing. The four young people made a substantial hole in the roof above where Jesus was standing in order to lower their friend through and, in doing so, they must inevitably have displaced a whole heap of building material onto the floor of the room below – and onto the people in that room as well.

You may say 'Well, when they realised what was happening the people below stepped aside'. Not so, for the house was crammed. This - the very reason the young men had to go up onto the roof at all - prevented those in the room below from escaping the falling debris. They were all packed in and there was no escape! In other words, a whole lot of rubbish fell on Jesus' godly head and, if he was wearing a long white robe as tradition would have us believe, then that too would have been covered in dirt. There was nothing he could do about it except to stand there in the falling rubble and watch the mat containing the sick young man being lowered down to him.

One can only imagine what happened then. The paralysed man was now looking straight into the eyes of God, who was covered from head to foot with muck as a result of what they had done. I see him staring, scared out of his wits and wide-eyed and I think he might have said something like 'Oh no!' and then 'boys, pull me up. I'm in deep trouble down here'. An uncomfortable moment passed while everyone strained to see what would happen next. And then, I believe, Jesus laughed. It was a huge laugh, a belly laugh. He laughed with tears streaming down his face mixing with the grime that covered him. Then he said 'friend, your sins are forgiven.' (Luke 5:20)

Here we have a wonderful picture of Jesus covered in debris, muck and grime because of this young man and his friends. Jesus was quite literally covered with their dirt. So no, he didn't say immediately 'get up and walk,' (Luke 5:23) because that was not what was required in the circumstances just then. What Jesus did was to meet the immediate need of this young man who needed forgiveness for covering him in muck.

However, not everyone was happy. The Pharisees and the teachers of the law were also in the room. These were important people who had also been unable to avoid the falling building material. Like Jesus, they were covered in muck – only they didn't laugh. In fact quite the opposite - they were quite put out. As far as they were concerned, these young men didn't deserve forgiveness. These hooligans had not only broken down the roof of the house, but they had covered their nice clothes with rubble.

So a gap opened up between young and old, as it so often does. But another gap was also forming between the Pharisees and Jesus because Jesus had the audacity to forgive the young people. The Pharisees represented the old wineskins. Their way of life could not tolerate change, and was centred on rules and blame. Does this not sound familiar to us in today's society? Any attempt to repair this culture would have been useless.

Jesus brought something new to replace this culture. He brought a new way, of forgiveness and reconciliation, and he showed it in this story in a very practical way. So after forgiving the young man for covering him in muck, he turned to meet the young man's next immediate need. He said '...get up, take your mat and go home,' (Luke 5:24). The young man got up and started a new life, free from his sickness, and I think that his four loyal friends did the same.

Old and new

Chapter five is about being able to change. It is about young and old, but has nothing to do with age. Young people can be old when they get caught up in a judgmental culture dictated by fashion, whilst old people can be at the most innovative and creative time of their lives. On the other hand old people can be blinkered from seeing the value of anything other than what they have known in the past, whilst the young are prepared to step out into the unknown.

The lesson of chapter five is that we must not convince ourselves that we can stay where we are. We must always be ready to accept something new from God. Jesus came into the world to free those who are stuck. As a boy, he probably learned a passage from Isaiah which stayed with him throughout his ministry. It says 'Forget the former things, don't dwell on the past. Behold - I am doing something new' (Isaiah 43:18-19). Chapter six tells us what's in store when we are prepared to become new.

CHAPTER SIX

MESS

My kingdom is not of this world. (John 18:36)

The Impossible was in the middle of a scrum! He was out in the country, surrounded by hundreds of people from all over central Palestine, and they all had one purpose...to touch him! These were the poor and needy, the desperate, the lonely, the sick, the prostitutes and the depressed, all reaching out to him because he could heal them. I don't think it was a particularly uplifting sight. Certainly it was unlike any church service or any other type of religious gathering that we might be used to. Rather, it was lots of people scrambling, pushing and shoving to get close.

I recall many years ago walking through a Neapolitan suburb. I had to walk through a gauntlet of children who followed, grabbing clothes and hands and shouting 'Money, money' – probably the only word of English that they knew. It wasn't a pleasant experience. They crowded around me and I shook them off - unlike Jesus, who allowed his crowd to fall over themselves to touch him. Jesus' heaven is very different from my world.

Blessings

Eventually some order was bought to the chaos out in the country that day, and the 'large crowd of his disciples' stepped back far enough for Jesus to deliver one of his great sermons, known as the Sermon on the Plain.

> Blessed are the poor
> Blessed are the hungry
> Blessed are those who weep
> Blessed are the insulted and the rejected
> (Adapted from Luke 6:20-22)

Those listening, the needy and the sick, will have seen themselves in these opening words. This was for them. Their spirits were raised as they heard him say 'rejoice in that day and leap for joy,' (Luke 6:23) and they responded with a loud cheer. So he went on with more -

> Woe to the rich
> Woe to the well fed
> Woe to those who think that this is all a laughing matter
> Woe to those who seek the company of yes men
> (Adapted from Luke 6:24-26)

'Go on Jesus, this is what we all want to hear' - and again an even bigger cheer, and they craned their necks and opened their ears to hear all that he would say next. What he then said was not what they were expecting. He said two things which must have silenced them. 'Love your enemies,' (Luke 6:27) was the first, and if this wasn't enough, he added a second: 'do not judge' (Luke 6:37). This would not have gone down well with those who craved for a champion.

Love your enemies?

This is new. This is as new to us today as it was when he said it. It is revolutionary. It turns their world, and our world, upside down. It's horribly confusing to us, because 'love' and 'enemies' are two words that don't sit comfortably with each other. It is as if Jesus is challenging them and us:

> 'You want new life?'
>   'Yes.'
> 'Freedom?'
>   'Yes!'
> 'OK. Then love your enemies'
>   'I can't.'
> 'Even if your worst enemy is yourself?'
>   'I still can't.'
> 'Then you are stuck in the same old clothes.'

'Jesus, what do you mean - love your enemies? Are you sure you have this right? There must be some confusion. You didn't really mean to say that did you?' Oh yes he did. Look, he goes on...

> Do good to those who hate you
> Bless those who curse you
> Pray for those who ill-treat you
> Be prepared for someone to hit you again
> Give your coat and then your shirt
> Do to others as you would have them do to you
> (Adapted from Luke 6:27-31)

So who is our enemy? Our enemy is whoever spitefully uses us. Our enemy hits us with words and actions and our enemy deprives us of what is ours. Our enemy does things and acts in a way that we don't like. He or she treats us in a way we don't wish and Jesus is telling us that an essential foundation of freedom is to love that enemy.

BUT I DON'T WANNA LOVE MY ENEMIES!!

And that is the difficulty that we are all in. The new life that Jesus offers is far removed from the old life. It's as far removed as God, the creator, is from us specks. Yet the freedom that we most want is to be found in the new life that Jesus offers to us. It is in this new life we will find God. As before, we are bought up against something which seems impossible.

Don't misunderstand this. He is not calling on any of us to be people pleasers. However, we may know someone who has let us down, or from whom we would have expected better, or someone who we trusted who has deceived us. Jesus' instruction to all of us is – love them. Love them in the same way as we would want others to continue loving us when we do something they don't like.

Do not judge?

As a consequence of loving our enemies, we must not judge others. Jesus says:

> *Do not judge and you will not be judged*
> *Do not condemn and you will not be condemned*

Forgive, and you will be forgiven (Luke 6:37)

The desire to judge others is so deeply imbued in each one of us. The old order of rules and judgment clings to us like an old coat we can't get rid of. From an ingrained sense of self-righteousness, we accuse and we condemn. Judging others is illustrated by two stories to be found at the beginning of the chapter. Just imagine going to church Sunday after Sunday and meeting this!

Last Sunday

'Excuse me Jesus, can I have a quiet word?'
　'Yes, what is it?'
'Look, do you think that you could get your disciples under control?'
　'Why? What have they done?'
'Well, they were seen walking through a cornfield and eating ears of corn.'
　'That was out of control?'
'Yes - they mustn't do that on the Sabbath'
　'You are joking, aren't you?' (Adapted from Luke 6:1-2)

This Sunday

'Sorry Jesus, but we have another problem.'
　'What - eating corn again?'
'No, it's about that man that you healed this morning.'
　'You mean the man with a withered hand?'
'Yes. You shouldn't do healing on the Sabbath. It's against God's rules.'
　'So it would be better that I did nothing, is that it?'
'Oh no! Healing is OK tomorrow or the next day - but not today.'
　'Are you for real?' (Adapted from Luke 6:6-8)

Doesn't it make your eyes roll to heaven! Yet judging others presents real problems for all today. Just try not judging others and see how hard it is not to do this, just for one hour. We are not helped by the media in this. Television in particular constantly demands that we judge others, whether they be politicians, celebrities or the parade of unhappy people who will do anything to get on the box, even at the cost of their self respect.

No one has found God through condemnation. No one has found freedom through hatred. No one has found God or gained freedom by judging others. Freedom is never found at the expense of others. When we set others free of our judgment, free of our hatred and of our condemnation, we effectively set ourselves free. That is what Jesus meant when he said:

> *Do not judge and you will not be judged. Do not condemn and you will not be condemned. Forgive and you will be forgiven. (Luke 6:37)*

Forgiveness

Forgiveness is the bedrock of a successful life. If we can forgive, then we will flourish. If we can't forgive, then we will die inside. I remember when I first found the bedrock of forgiveness in my life. It was over a very small and insignificant incident. I was in my office with one of my staff, and we had work-related problems. Into the office walked my boss. He had problems. Then into my office a few moments later walked the big boss, and he had problems as well. My office was filled with people with problems, all demanding my attention. At that point the phone rang. It was someone called Chris, who had a knack of ringing me at awkward times. 'I can't talk to you now, Chris,' I said, but he insisted, and went on until I had to tell him that I was going to hang up on him. He continued, so I hung up. Moments later Chris was back on the phone again. 'You hung up on me!' he protested. 'Yes,' I said, and put the phone down a second time. I was furious. On the way home I reflected on the incident, saw the funny side and forgave him. I knew that when I saw Chris again he would have a go at me - and I wasn't wrong - but my forgiveness had worked. Chris had no claim on me and I was free of my anger. We parted amicably.

Of course there are much larger issues, which might cause greater obstacles to forgiveness. It is, however, even more important to forgive the larger issues if we are not to live the remainder of our lives in bitterness. Yet many, very sadly, hang on to old scores, priding themselves in their stubbornness deeming it to be the foundation of their strength. Instead they become like old sacks which burst apart when they are used and filled.

As they crucified him, Jesus said, 'Father, forgive them, for they do not know what they are doing,' (Luke 23:34).

The wise and foolish builders

Jesus knew that the concept of loving one's enemies, not judging others, and forgiveness would be difficult to grasp. So he finished his sermon with an illustration. It is a very familiar story about two men each building a house.

> *As for those who come to me and hear my words and put them into practice, I will show you what they are like. They are like a man building a house, who dug down deep and laid the foundation on rock. When a flood came, the torrent struck that house but could not shake it, because it was well built. But those who hear my words and do not put them into practice are like a man who built a house on the ground without a foundation. The moment the torrent struck that house, it collapsed and its destruction was complete. (Luke 6:47-49)*

We are to imagine two similar houses, representing our lives, being erected side by side. The ground conditions are not enough to support either house because the bedrock is too far down. The builder of the first house surveys the site and tests the ground conditions. He realises that the ground won't support the weight of the building so, as part of the foundations, he drives two vertical shafts into the ground until they reach the bedrock below. It is an expensive operation and takes a long time to complete; and in the meantime, the site is muddy and very messy. Nevertheless, although there are problems on the way, the house is completed and has been tested against some adverse weather conditions. The ground conditions might be weak, but the supports are in place and the house stands.

The builder of the second house also surveys the site and tests the ground conditions. He is prepared to gamble that the ground conditions are sufficient to bear the weight of the construction. The house, without those two vertical shafts, would be half the cost and would be built in half the time. Furthermore, his building site is far less messy. However, after completion, adverse weather conditions produce some alarming cracks in the walls, and evidence of subsidence is clear. The builder is faced with a choice. Either he has to demolish and start again or he has to underpin. Either way the problem is catastrophic.

With this illustration, the message from the sermon becomes clear. If our lives are carefully constructed on the teaching of Jesus, then we will be able to withstand the storms that will inevitably rage around us. We must drive two supports into the bedrock of our lives. The first support is 'love your enemies', and the second is 'don't judge others'. Get these into place resting on the bedrock of forgiveness and we will be able to stand in adversity.

But the construction is not easy, and it cannot be done too quickly. It takes time to get used to loving our enemies. It takes time and cost as we find ourselves judging others. Yet all the time that we're in a mess getting it wrong, and learning from our mistakes, these two supports are being driven in deeper and deeper.

So Jesus started his sermon in a mess and he finished it with a mess. He started with the sight of an unseemly scramble of people trying to touch him and finished with a muddy building site. Through it all we are asked to look at ourselves. What kind of construction supports the 'house' of our lives? Do we look good but know deep down that cracks are appearing? Or are we building on foundations of love and acceptance based on forgiveness, in spite of the fact that at times we look a mess and get it wrong?

A prayer:

Jesus, Peter said 'go away from me, for I am a sinful man' (Luke 5:8). We kneel before you, as Peter did, like a messy building site. We reach out to you, scramble to you, for only your touch can give us what we need. Only through you can we dig deep foundations so that we can stand through the worst of storms. Only through you can we find God.

CHAPTER SEVEN

OUT OF MESS COMES GREATNESS

The greatest among you will be your servant. For those who exalt themselves will be humbled, and those who humble themselves will be exalted. (Matthew 23:11,12)

Jesus had preached the Sermon on the Plain. He told us that building the foundations of our lives is a messy business. We get it wrong time and again, which is why we must not judge and condemn others - for they are probably constructing their lives in just as much mess as we are. After the Sermon on the Plain, there are four wonderful stories of people like us whose lives were in a mess.

The first is the story of a centurion and his sick servant. Out of the mess, the centurion emerged with great faith. This is followed by the story of a widow who lived in a village called Nain, whose son had died. Out of her sorrowful mess emerged great joy. The third is the story about a message that Jesus received from John the Baptist who was now in prison. In imprisonment the greatest man born of woman was affirmed by the one he came to herald. The chapter finishes with the painful story of a sinful woman who anointed Jesus' feet. Out of her great sin was brought great acceptance.

In each case their lives were in a mess; yet each one emerged with some form of greatness.

The centurion and his great faith

Gaius Cassandro (we'll call him) commanded one of the six centuries that made up the cohort based at Capernaum. We might imagine him as a rough man who ate, slept and fought alongside the 80 legionnaires that made up his century. He was serving his twenty-first year in the Roman army. With only five years before retirement, his legion was posted to Galilee, a region in Palestine. Cassandro didn't hesitate and obeyed orders instantly and that is why he was a centurion.

He knew enough about army occupation in a foreign country to realise that you didn't get the best results by bullying the natives. Sometimes he wished he could ring the scrawny necks of some of those pompous religious leaders in Capernaum but, in his rough way, he treated them fairly. When he arrived at Capernaum a few years ago, he found that the synagogue had been gutted by fire. He suggested, to the surprise of the Jewish elders, that he build another one. He put his 80 legionnaires to work and made friends with the locals all at the same time. Cassandro was no fool.

Fool or not, Cassandro had a problem. His servant was sick. This servant wasn't just any servant. Not only did he look after Cassandro's horse and his equipment, but he kept him informed about what was happening within the century. Also he seemed to know everything about what was happening in Capernaum. His loyal servant would wake him, get him where he had to be, feed him and, at times, collect him from drunken nights out, take him home and put him to bed. Now, this servant was sick and close to dying. Cassandro didn't know what to do. In fact he could do nothing. He just sat by his servant's bed – helpless.

Then some of the Jewish elders came to him with some news. It seemed that there was a prophet there in Capernaum called Jesus. He had healed the paralysed and lepers. 'I wonder,' thought Cassandro, 'could he heal my servant?' No one had any other suggestions to make and, as one of the elders was a scribe, he sent a message through him:

GAIUS CASSANDRO TO JESUS OF NAZARETH, GREETINGS.
SERVANT SICK. WILL DIE BEFORE NIGHTFALL. PLEASE CURE.
HAIL CAESAR.

The Jewish elders took the message to Jesus. They pleaded with him to come and told Jesus what the centurion had done for them. Jesus dictated a response.

JESUS OF NAZARETH TO GAIUS CASSANDRO. ACKNOWLEDGED
SERVANT SICK. AM ON MY WAY. GLORY TO GOD

When Cassandro received the message from Jesus, he was nonplussed. This was not what he expected. He didn't anticipate that Jesus would actually come to him. The place was a mess. These were soldier's quarters for goodness sake! So he asked the scribe to take a further message to Jesus.

> GAIUS CASSANDRO TO JESUS OF NAZARETH. SIR, NO NEED TO
> TROUBLE YOURSELF TO COME HERE. GIVE ORDERS AND
> SERVANT WILL BE WELL. HAIL CAESAR

Now it was Jesus' turn to be taken aback. Never before had he seen anything like this. This was the greatest faith that he had found. His response:

> JESUS OF NAZARETH TO GAIUS CASSANDRO. IT IS DONE. GLORY
> TO GOD.

And the servant was well when the Jewish elders returned.

The sick servant

Give a thought to the centurion's sick servant, as he lay dying. He didn't know when he started feeling ill. He thought the spells of dizziness would pass. He had been through worse. Then one day he became very tired and had difficulty standing on his feet. At first he was afraid because he was letting his master down, but the centurion was concerned. The servant was ordered to bed and, as he lay there, he wondered how his master would cope without him. Then others were in the room talking amongst themselves and looking at him as he lapsed into fever.

Then he awoke. He was quite alone and it was quiet and wondered for a moment whether he had died and gone to Hades. But he didn't feel dead, in fact he felt quite well. Gingerly he got up. The fever had gone, his legs were firm and there was no sign of dizziness. Standing there, the servant hadn't a clue what had been going on around him.

The story of the centurion and his sick servant has much to tell us today. Things happen and we don't know why. We are totally unaware of the prayers of faith that are being said for us in the way that the centurion and the Jewish elders were praying to Jesus. Across the world prayers are being said for others. Many of these prayers are said without knowing the result. Many results are known without realising why. This is the faith of Christians in the Impossible. This was the great faith of a poor centurion who could do nothing and so turned to Jesus.

That night, Cassandro was in heaven. Heaven is where all things are well and all was well with Cassandro that night. He was so happy he went to the wine bars of Capernaum and got thoroughly drunk. As had happened many times before, his loyal servant took him home and put him to bed.

> *Blessed are you who are poor, for yours is the kingdom of God (Luke 6:20)*

The widow of Nain

She had no further reason to live. All that was precious had been taken away - first her husband and now her son, her only son. She was well-respected in the little town of Nain. Her grief was theirs. Like the centurion they were all poor in the sense that they could do nothing. Her poverty was her hunger for what she had lost, and now she had to bury the only person who mattered in her life. That day they carried him, supposedly for the last time, took him to the burial place outside the town and she followed until they reached the town gate of Nain.

In the meantime, Jesus was walking away from Capernaum towards the little town of Nain. His head was still spinning with the faith that he had found in the centurion that he had never met. One day soon, another centurion would put his faith in him at the Place of the Skull, as he saw Jesus die. However, right now it seemed he could never go anywhere quietly. Soon, he and his disciples were being joined by others. Many had heard about him, and tagged along to see what he would do next. They were not to be disappointed. There was never a dull moment with Jesus. And then they reached the town gate of Nain.

So on one side of the gate of Nain was a crowd of mourners following a woman and her dead son, whilst on the other side of the gate of Nain was another crowd, lively and expecting something great to happen. At the gate of Nain, these two large crowds met and mingle around two people alone in the world – a poor, spiritually famished woman, and the Impossible. For what Jesus did then was impossible for anyone other than him.

He saw her
His heart went out to her
He touched the coffin as if he touched her heart
He said to her 'don't weep'
He said to the dead man 'get up'
He spoke to the living and the dead equally
And then he gave her son, now alive, back to her
(Adapted from Luke 7:13-15)

There is something significant about the gate of Nain. Imagine that you are like the crowd that mingled together. Part of the crowd was expecting something wonderful to happen while another part was mourning. Isn't that like us? Aren't there days when we feel the heaviness of mourning, while on other days we are excited with anticipation? So which side of the gate of Nain are we on right now? There is no right side or wrong side. We are what we are - sometimes heavy, sometimes light; but whatever side we are on right now, Jesus is at the gate, ready to receive us.

But there is another way of looking at the gate of Nain. We have a choice. Do we go through the gate and meet Jesus, or do we hold back? The widow, who had lost her son, went through the gate in her great sorrow and met Jesus. Had she not done so, she would have remained in her hunger. If we, the hungry, are prepared to do the same, if we are prepared to go and meet with Jesus, his heart will go out to us, as it did to her. That is what this wonderful story is about.

Blessed are you who hunger now, for you will be satisfied
(Luke 6:21)

A message from John the Baptist

Another group of messengers arrived. Jesus might well have felt his heart lift as they were messengers from his friend John (that is, John the Baptist). But what they had to say would have dampened any spirit.

Are you the one who was to come, or should we expect someone else?
(Luke 7:19)

John was in prison, and soon to die. He was a leader of men whose life was in crisis, like a house in a storm rocking on its foundations. He had expected so much, yet it didn't seem to be working out. No doubt his disciples had reported back to John what Jesus had said on the plain. 'Love your enemies,' they heard Jesus say, 'do not judge'. They, like everybody else, were taken by surprise. John had worked so hard. His message was tough, as tough as the desert he lived in; yet it seemed he was getting nowhere. Now, as he lay incarcerated and helpless, his hope in Jesus was evaporating. Perhaps he had been wrong after all.

John represents all leaders. This has a message for us, particularly when our 'house' is being rocked by storms raging against it. This is for leaders who feel that they are getting nowhere and can't seem to get anything right. Enthusiasm is worn down and worn out.

They weep, as many weep, over the spiritual poverty of our nation and feel helpless to do anything about it.

It is at times like this that Jesus seems far removed. Some leaders are beset with doubts, as John was. When we feel this way, we might think of sending 'messengers' to Jesus like John and the centurion did - people who can be trusted to pray for us and help us find what Jesus wants us to do. Jesus will not criticise us any more than he criticised John. Instead he will pour out the warmth of his praise to all who have been faithful to their calling as he did to John. The time of weeping will pass and a time of laughter will follow.

Blessed are you who weep now, for you will laugh. (Luke 6:21)

The sinful woman

Perhaps she was a prostitute. How did it happen? The simple truth was that she needed money. The simple truth was that she had made some bad errors in her life. The simple truth is that there was no simple truth. She loved men and she hated them all at the same time. Then one day she decided to follow the crowd out into the country and, on a plain, she found herself around a man who was like no other man she had ever met. She couldn't explain it – she just wanted to touch him, but the trouble was, so did everyone else. Everybody was pushing and shoving to get near him. Try as she might, it was impossible to get near.

That night she went home disappointed but still with a desire to touch him. Then she heard that he was to be invited to Simon the Pharisee's house, and a plan started to take shape in her mind. Getting into the house while they were having dinner was not a problem. She had been in and out of that house more times than she could remember. Her problem was what to do when she got there. Would Jesus accept her touching him? Then she saw the jar of perfume on the shelf. This was her only valuable possession. She wouldn't part with that jar for the world but now...perhaps now was the time to put it to use.

On the day of the dinner, she went to the house of the Pharisee. Her heart was pounding as she clasped the alabaster jar close to her chest. She smiled at the doorkeeper, who grinned back. When she entered the room they were all reclining and at first she couldn't see Jesus. But they all saw her. There was a stunned silence, which was then broken by a raucous male cheer. 'Who have you come to entertain today, darling?' called one. She ignored them and saw Jesus. If he was alarmed as she stood by his feet, he didn't show it. With shaking hands, she took out the alabaster jar. 'Keep calm,' she kept telling herself, but instead she broke down, falling to her knees and massaging tears and perfume into his feet.

Self righteousness then re-asserted itself. It took a little time for the men to recover their dignity as they watched incredulously at the spectacle. 'This is a disgrace,' protested the man who had previously jeered her. She had come to pour out her broken life. In doing so she was condemned by those around the dinner table - not because she was a prostitute, but because she, a prostitute, had the audacity to turn to Jesus.

> *Blessed are you when people hate you, when they exclude you and insult you and reject your name as evil because of the Son of Man. (Luke 6:22)*

This is for all sinners, particularly anyone who has brought distress to others. It is for anyone who has caused offence, yet still turns to Jesus. 'Do not judge,' said Jesus on the plain to those gathered around. He meant it for them and he means it today, for Christians and non-believers alike. The men at that dinner hated the woman. They insulted her and were intent on excluding her. We must take care not to do the same. We must take an honest look and see when and who we are guilty of judging. Such judgment will only bring judgment back.

Jesus does not condemn. So instead, he turned to the woman who had sinned greatly and forgave her sins and he will do the same for anyone who has the audacity to turn to him in their sinfulness. He also added one last thing. He said to the woman, 'your faith has saved you; go in peace' (Luke 7:50). So she left that house forgiven, and her faith stood on firm foundations alongside a rough centurion, a widowed mother and John the Baptist. In one way or another, their lives were in a mess. Yet each emerged with greatness, and with lives whose very foundations were built on bedrock of forgiveness.

CHAPTER EIGHT

SEED HAVE NO LEGS

For there is nothing hidden that will not be disclosed... (Luke 8:17)

Up to now we have been like bystanders. First we witnessed the period of Jesus' birth, from the shepherds on a hillside to John the Baptist in the desert. Then we witnessed the formation of his ministry, in the wilderness. We then discovered through the Sermon on the Plain that the foundations of our lives are to be constructed on two great shafts - loving our enemies and not judging others, both shafts resting on the bedrock of forgiveness. Now, in chapter eight, there is a change of emphasis. No longer are we allowed to be bystanders. It is as if Luke suddenly turns the light on each one of us with the unspoken question: 'where are you with all this?' Jesus tells us in the chapter that no one lights a lamp and puts it under a bed (Luke 8:16). Instead, he puts it on a stand for all to see, and it is this light that now shines gently on us, seeking us out.

So the light comes onto us now through a very well known parable. Perhaps it is too well known, too familiar, but I want to try to look at it with new eyes.

The parable of the sower

> *A farmer went out to sow his seed. As he was scattering the seed, some fell along the path; it was trampled on, and the birds ate it up. Some fell on rock, and when it came up, the plants withered because they had no moisture. Other seed fell among thorns, which grew up with it and choked the plants. Still other seed fell on good soil. It came up and yielded a crop, a hundred times more than was sown. (Luke 8:5-8)*

This is clearly a parable that Jesus wants each of us to understand, so he gives us an explanation:

69

This is the meaning of the parable: The seed is the word of God. Those along the path are the ones who hear, and then the devil comes and takes away the word from their hearts, so that they may not believe and be saved. Those on the rock are the ones who receive the word with joy when they hear it, but they have no root. They believe for a while, but in the time of testing they fall away. The seed that fell among thorns stands for those who hear, but as they go on their way they are choked by life's worries, riches and pleasures, and they do not mature. But the seed on good soil stands for those with a noble and good heart, who hear the word, retain it, and by persevering produce a crop. (Luke 8:11-15)

Are we taking on board what God is saying to us through the first chapters of this gospel? What sort of ground does our seed lie on? We might reply with some of these thoughts quietly to ourselves:

Thought one – I might not understand or even have faith in God's word, but that doesn't mean that I'm a shallow person. I think deeply about what I read and hear so I don't think that I am like the first two grounds where the seed fell on the path or on the rocks.

Thought two - If I'm really honest, sometimes I can be like the ground full of thorns. I can be like that third seed because sometimes I do tend to let worries overtake me.

Thought three - Well, I think that I have a good heart and that people benefit from my friendship so I would like to think that I am the good ground that the seed fell on (well mostly anyway).

My own answer would have followed along these rather woolly lines. For years I have answered this question - albeit half-consciously – by thinking 'I have my problems and at times I feel choked with worry, but I try to get onto the good ground as much as I can'
Then an awful truth hit me about this parable – seed have no legs.

It occurred to me that Jesus was very purposeful in selecting seed as his illustration. Seed are absolutely powerless to move. Where they lie is where they are. They can't suddenly sprout legs, get off the path where they fell and into the good ground, even if that good ground is only inches away. Seed are stuck where they fall.

We are equally stuck. We are stuck in the ground that we are on as much as the seed is stuck. If we are choked by the thorns of worry, then that is the ground that we are in. We cannot move ourselves to the good ground, any more than the seed has legs.

This agonising truth of our helplessness has been preached and written about many times. However, in spite of this there always seems to remain a lingering thought in the minds of many, including myself, that somehow we can get ourselves into the good ground and therefore into a right position with God. This cannot be done. It is impossible. Only when we realise the helplessness of our position in front of God can we truly understand why Jesus came into the world. Only then can we realise that only Jesus can make possible what is impossible for us, and only then will we realise how futile it is to judge others who are just as helpless.

Knowing this, we must ask ourselves that question again – where are we in this parable? What ground are we on? If we are to find an answer to this, we must be truly open and honest with ourselves. We must allow Jesus' gentle light to shine through us so that nothing will be concealed. If we look at Luke chapter eight we will see that the parable of the sower is followed by four stories. Four seeds followed by four stories. Observe how each story has been placed carefully in the order of the four seeds.

The seed on the path	The story of Jesus' mother and brothers
The seed on the rock	The story of Jesus calming the storm
The seed in the thorns	The story of Jesus healing the demon-possessed man
The seed on the good ground	The story of Jairus and the sick woman

Perhaps we might look at each story and see which one has most to say to us. The answers produced might be quite shocking; but I must emphasise that my aim with this is not to shock or to offend, but to make us think about exactly where we are in this parable. We might turn out not to have the relationship with God that we might think we have; conversely, we might have a relationship with God that we were not aware we had.

The story of Jesus' mother and brothers: the seed on the path

We read that Jesus' mother and brothers came to see him but were prevented from getting to him because of the crowd. We have seen from Luke's gospel that this seems to be a regular occurrence - only unlike the other instances where this had happened, Jesus' family felt that they had a right to see him. They were, after all, his mother and brothers! There is something about those words 'they are wanting to see you,' (Luke 8:20) that creates an atmosphere of ownership. Yet they were left outside.

Now surely Jesus' mother and brothers represent the good soil, don't they? Yet they were dismissed – even curtly dismissed - by Jesus. On being told that his mother and brothers were waiting for him, Jesus replies 'my mother and brothers are those who hear God's word and put it into practice,' (Luke 8:21). In Mark's version of the story, he adds 'Who are my mother and brothers?' (Mark 3:33). His family thought that they had some pre-emptive right over Jesus, and in fact they had no right at all.

Theirs is the seed that falls on the path, seed that was trampled on and gobbled up in a moment, just as the seed on the path was gobbled by the birds. This seed represents those people whose thoughts are blinkered by unsupported assumptions about Jesus - and it is shocking and unthinkable that this might apply to his mother and brothers. But if it applies to them, how much more does it apply to us?

We hear God's word but then something gets in the way.

The story of Jesus calming the storm: the seed on the rock

The second story attaches itself more obviously to the second seed. The second seed fell on the rock and withered in the sun with no moisture. The second story, however, had no lack of moisture, as it was about Jesus calming the storm. Again, we might think that the disciples should have been good soil but, under the stress of the storm, they withered as assuredly as the second seed withered.

Yet they, the disciples, had followed Jesus. 'Let us go over to the other side of the lake,' (Luke 8:22) said Jesus. Obediently they went and were overcome by the storm. They folded under the storm of a life crisis, particularly when they realised that Jesus was asleep.

We hear God's word to us but then it is swept away by fear.

The story of the demon possessed man: the seed among thorns

The third story is about a poor demented man living naked among the tombs, totally out of his mind. Jesus healed him by driving out the demons that possessed him. Luke writes that he drove the demons into a herd of pigs which then destroyed themselves. When the pig-tenders told the pig-owners what had happened, they were not at all happy and protested without much care for the man who had regained his senses.

This story illustrates the third type of ground where the seed was scattered – that is, the seed that fell among thorns that choke them. These thorns represent the worry that consumes many. A few years ago I met a man in my workplace. He was self-confident and was likeable, if a little arrogant in a 21st century sort of way. I met him again more recently. By now recession had struck, and he was clinging to his job by his fingernails. His self-confidence seemed to be in tatters, his morale low as he looked around himself, scared that someone might hear us talking. His underlying fear was being overheard by those who employed him. He felt he was held in no higher regard than the pig-owners had for the demented man who lived with the dead.

We may not see ourselves as being like the demented man until we realise that much of our life is spent feeling vulnerable and naked as we ponder our future, our family, our financial stability and our mortality.

We hear God's word but then worry consumes it.

The story of Jairus and the sick woman: the seed on good soil

Finally to the good soil - the soil to which we might aspire. The fourth story, which represents the good soil, is about two people who are utterly broken, like good soil is broken. There was a sick woman with an embarrassing condition which left her a social outcast as well as feeling extremely uncomfortable. She came up behind Jesus weeping rather like the prostitute had done in the Pharisee's house (see chapter seven). She wanted to touch Jesus as the prostitute had also wanted to touch him. As always it had to be done in a crowd. She couldn't touch his feet but she did manage to touch his robe. She was a very private figure and we don't even know her name.

The other was Jairus. He was quite the opposite to the woman. Jairus was a very public figure, being leader of the synagogue, and we do know his name. Yet he was as broken as the anonymous woman. His brokenness came through an illness that had afflicted his daughter, who was now close to dying. He had attracted Jesus' attention, and he had agreed to come with him to his house and to his dying daughter. However, Jairus had to exercise huge self-control when everything was interrupted by the emergence of this anonymous woman. Oh the frustration of it! Yet this public and important man graciously and patiently waited while Jesus stopped and enquired about who it was that had just touched him. She was identified and bought to the front of the whole crowd so that all could see that she was healed.

When, at last, they reached Jairus' house, it was seemingly too late. His little girl had died. Yet Jairus voiced no condemnation on Jesus or on the anonymous woman. He didn't voice any thought that his daughter might have lived had Jesus not delayed. Silently, he accepted Jesus' assurance: 'don't be afraid, just believe and she will be healed' (Luke 8:50). With that, Jesus took Peter, James and John with him into the house and, with them alone, he healed Jairus' daughter.

These two very different people are the good soil. There wasn't a shred of arrogance in either of them, both of them were riding a storm and both were choked by grief. Neither thought they possessed anything, yet, in Jesus, both possessed everything they needed. One very private lady was healed very publicly while one very public man had a daughter who was healed very privately.

Theirs was the kingdom of heaven.

Replanted

How can we get onto the good ground if we are so helpless? How are we able to get God's word into our very being and thrive on it? The answer is that we can't do this by ourselves. So if the seed can't move, then the only alternative is that the ground around the seed has to move.

This is what happens when the ground beneath our feet is churned up. The rocks of our security are smashed, the weeds of our world are uprooted, and our seed is effectively replanted. This happened to Jairus in the illness and death of his daughter. It happened to the woman with the embarrassing illness. Both saw Jesus as very relevant to their changing lives.

When our lives are overturned, all our previous values seem to count for nothing, as we look forwards in an entirely different way. From now on nothing will be the same. At times like this, Jesus can become very relevant to us as we put aside all previously held prejudices. We look back and realise that something new was born in that stormy moment. King David wrote a Psalm after his life had been turned upside down that summed it all up:

> My sacrifice, O God, is a broken spirit;
> a broken and contrite heart
> you, God, will not despise (Psalm 51:17)

Where are we with all this? The gentle light of Jesus is on a stand, illuminating our answer for both God and us to see. The good ground is found in broken hearts, and those people most effectively take the word of God to others. Tears and laughter are never far away as they minister their love to all going through the highs and lows of life. Sometimes their efforts to take the word of God to others goes wrong and, in their brokenness, they learn from their failures. On other times they get it right, bearing 'a crop a hundred times more than was sown' (Luke 8:8). We shall see both failure and success in the following two chapters.

Part Three: On the road to Jerusalem

CHAPTER NINE

FAILURE – STEPPING FORWARD

Jesus resolutely set out for Jerusalem (Luke 9:51)

In business there is an 'f' word that no one mentions. The word that I am referring to is 'failure'. Use this word in any business meeting, and you will see it reduced to stunned silence as minds around the table contemplate the competence of the person who had the audacity to say it. Yet, if we think about it for a moment, it is clear that we cannot have success without failure. Success and failure go hand in hand – it's like breathing in and breathing out. If we only accept success, it is rather like breathing in all the time. If we were to do this, we would die - and that is what happens to those who refuse to come to terms with failure. They literally die inside.

It is at times of failure that we take our biggest strides forward because it is then that we can learn – but only if we allow ourselves to learn. I believe that Jesus knew this as he assembled his motley crew of twelve disciples together. It was time for their training to begin as he prepared them to go out into a wanting and hostile world. It was to be their first attempt at mission and it would end in failure but, in the course of that failure, they would learn. So Jesus gathered them together.

> Men, up to now you have been following me. You have seen me drive out demons and cure diseases, and now it's your turn. I am giving you authority to preach the kingdom of God and to heal the sick.
> OK Jesus, what do we need to take with us?
> Absolutely nothing - only my authority.
> What about food and money?
> Allow people to provide for you, and if they don't, then shake their dust off your shoes.
> (Adapted from Luke 9:1-6)

I don't think it is hard to imagine their reaction. I think that they would have felt rather vulnerable and unprepared going from village to village, a bit like trainees might feel when first let loose on a job. But if they were going to have any chance of success they would need to be absolutely confident of who Jesus was. Without that, preaching the kingdom of God would be impossible, and healing the sick even more impossible. So he sat them down and asked them one of the most important questions that they had to answer. But, as ever, this question is not just for them – it's for us too. Who do the crowds say that I am? (Luke 9:18)

> Who do they say that I am?
> Well Jesus, that's tough one...
> Well come on!
> Well, some say that you are John the Baptist, but that really can't be possible, can it?
> Anything else?

Others say that you are Elijah, except you don't seem to scare so easily as Elijah did.

Any more?

Others say that you are a prophet of old but weren't too sure which one.

OK! OK! Enough of them. What about you? Who do you say that I am?

(Adapted from Luke 9:18-20)

And at that point Peter jumped in with 'God's Messiah' (Luke 9:20)

Peter steps forward

Peter had gone through a period of deep inner questioning. The realisation of who Jesus was did not come to him in a flash. We think of Peter blurting out answers – but he didn't blurt this one out. It was a gradual dawning that took its time, and it seems from Luke's account that it might have happened in three phases:

The dawn of his realisation. It started for Peter shortly after Jesus appeared out of the wilderness, when Jesus healed his mother-in-law enabling her to make the supper for them all (chapter four). He realised that there was something different about Jesus.

Peter's realisation about himself. Peter's realisation continued on Lake Gennesaret (chapter 5) where Jesus had dumbfounded him through the catch of fish even though he, Peter the expert fisherman, had caught nothing the night before. The realisation dawned on Peter about himself that he was nothing, a mere speck, by comparison to Jesus.

His realisation about Jesus. 'You are God's Messiah,' he said. This man was the Wonderful Counsellor that he had heard was to come; this man was Mighty God here in the world; this man was the Everlasting Father; this man was the Prince of Peace. This man had come to make it possible to have a relationship between Peter and the creator of the universe. Did Peter realise all this right then? Unlikely. He saw but a poor reflection, but when he said 'You are the Christ of God', he and the other disciples passed a milestone in their journey with Jesus.

However, their understanding was far from complete, and they didn't understand what Jesus said next. He told them that he was to go to Jerusalem and must suffer many things, and be rejected and killed - and on the third day be raised to life (Luke 9:22). But he also told them not to tell anyone (Luke 9:21). Why not tell anyone? Because Jesus was following one of the golden rules that he never broke. He was waiting for the 'nod from God'. It hadn't come yet but it was about to arrive.

Jesus steps forward

Jesus was about to come face to face with God the Father, on the Mount of Transfiguration. He left the disciples to their mission and took Peter, John and James with him up the mountain. Luke tells us;

> As he was praying, the appearance of his face changed, and his clothes became as bright as a flash of lightning. Two men, Moses and Elijah, appeared in glorious splendour, talking with Jesus. They spoke about his departure, which he was about to bring to fulfilment at Jerusalem. (Luke 9:29-31)

It's my belief that this is what Jesus had been waiting for. Now there was full understanding about his mission. Now he could resolutely set out for Jerusalem (Luke 9:51). But like Peter, realisation might have come in stages.

The dawn of realisation. There came a time when Jesus understood that there was something different about him. He was unique in the eyes of God and man. This realisation may have come from what his mother had told him about his birth. Certainly realisation dawned on both him and his mother over the incident in the temple when he was a boy (chapter two).

Jesus' realisation about himself as a man. As the boy became a man, he clearly had the means to study both Law and Prophets. The gospels are at one regarding his knowledge. I believe he understood his purpose, if not his destiny, when he emerged out of the wilderness. It seems to me that he knew his purpose when, in Nazareth, he declared that Isaiah's scripture would be fulfilled through him (chapter four).

His realisation about God. On the Mount of Transfiguration, God spoke to Jesus publicly again. God repeated what he had said at his baptism. 'This is my Son, whom I have chosen, listen to him,' (Luke 9:35). Jesus, having been aware of his purpose and destiny, now knew that nothing could restrain him not even death. The cross, the tomb and the resurrection were waiting for him. God had pressed the green light.

Disappointment and success

Meanwhile, back on the ground, things were not going well. The mission of the twelve had stalled. After an encouraging start, and in spite of having received Jesus' authority, the mission had flopped into a chapter of disappointment.

Jesus had been up the mountain with Peter, James and John and had been gloriously transfigured - but now he returned to bedlam! A large crowd met him with the furious father of a boy suffering from severe convulsions and the disciples could do nothing. Oh the disappointment that Jesus felt! He literally dropped from the heights of the mountain to the very depths of his soul. His frustration was very clear. 'How long will I stay with you and put up with you?' (Luke 9:41), he barked at them before healing the boy himself. Jesus was angry. 'The Son of Man is going to be betrayed,' (Luke 9:44) he warned. Yes, he felt the pain of failure in their betrayal of trust in him. They betrayed him by their unbelief, which resulted in them not being able to heal the boy. It was a foretaste of the betrayal that he would suffer at the hands of Judas on the Mount of Olives.

If that wasn't enough, Jesus was then entertained by an unseemly row between the disciples. The debate was a pathetic attempt to cover up their failure as they argued between themselves over who would be the greatest among them. Rather than becoming aware of their helpless position before God, they argued over who was the best! The disciples were acting no better than little boys of school age, so Jesus took a child and used him as an example. 'He who is least among you – he is the greatest,' (Luke 9:48) he said, pointing to the child. Had they been with Jesus and not learned this lesson?

Failure mounted upon failure. Jesus found that not even the premier league of disciples had learned anything. Peter was back to usual form when he displayed appalling insensitivity on the Mount of Transfiguration, when all he could do was blurt out tactless remarks while Jesus was adjusting himself to the confirmed realisation that he was to die a terrible and painful death. And then, a little later, James and John fared no better when in a fit of pique they suggested to Jesus that he rain down fire on a Samaritan village after they had been refused entry. It was a suggestion that bore no relationship to Jesus' exhortation to love their enemies and not judge anyone – even Samaritans!

The one bright spot – the feeding of the 5000

There was one bright spot in the mission - but this was because of Jesus, not because of the disciples. The story of the feeding of the 5000 is well known. People flocked to Jesus, trying to get close so that that they could hear him and be healed by him. Whether their gathering was as undignified as before, I don't know, but they were most certainly unprepared. No one had thought to bring any food. They were hungry and all they could find were five loaves of bread and two fish.

Jesus had the answer. 'You give them something to eat,' (Luke 9:13) he said to his disciples, as if he was thinking 'come on, I have commissioned you – now do it'. But they had no answers and, faced with their hopelessness, Jesus took control and fed them all.

We might find a crumb of comfort in knowing that the disciples could get it just as wrong as we do. How many of us make plans only to find our ideas crumbling into dust? Perhaps we should not get too despondent with our failure, and instead look at these times as periods of training. In training, we try to say the right things, only to find that we have put our foot in it. In training, we try not to judge others, only to find ourselves wishing that the person who is causing us grief would blow up in smoke! The twelve disciples got it wrong as we get it wrong, so we are in good company. Yet there is one thing we can depend on. While we are in training and making a hash of things, Jesus is there providing what we need so that next time we might get it right.

And the next time the disciples would get it right. They didn't know that success was just around the corner. They were about to leave failure behind and take with them the valuable truths that they had learned.

A step forward for us

So we come back to us again – we who get it wrong so often. Like the disciples we need to bounce back from failure because success is within our grasp. However, if we are to trust Jesus with this, we have to be absolutely sure in our hearts just who Jesus is. Furthermore, we need to know what he thinks about us. So imagine with me if you would, that we are talking with Jesus as the disciples talked to him and that he asks us the same question that he asked his disciples. This is how I think the conversation might go. It's not particularly *my* conversation; but perhaps we might use this as a template for whatever conversation might take place.

Jesus asks - who do people say that I am?

We reply - some say that you are a good man. Others say that you are a great teacher. Others think you are irrelevant; but most know you only as a swear word.

Jesus follows with a second question - OK, but who do you say that I am?

We reply - Jesus, you are the Christ of God

Now I want to open up this thought a bit further as we continue this conversation with Jesus. This time you ask him the same question back.

Jesus, can I ask you the same question? Who do people say that I am?

Jesus replies - some say that you are honest. Others say that you are a workaholic. Some say that you are obsessed with appearances. Some say you are faithful while others say that you are an adulterer. Some say that you are eaten up with jealousy.

Jesus, I need to follow that question with another. Who do you say that I am?

Jesus replies – you are a child of God!

You and I must put our own words in the conversation. But whichever way our conversation goes, the realisation that Jesus is the Christ of God brings with it Jesus' recognition that we are Children of God. When we come to understand this, we also pass a milestone as Peter and the disciples did.

He resolutely set out for Jerusalem

Jesus was aware of his destiny, and now he 'resolutely set out for Jerusalem.' He wouldn't be alone. The twelve would follow and he would pick up many on the way. Perhaps we might imagine that we are one of those that he picks us up on the way.

Listen, I want you to follow me.
OK Jesus, I will go with you where you go.
We start now.
So soon?
Any problems with that?
Well...it's just that I will have to tell my family what I'm doing...
Like I said. We start now.
Give me until tomorrow morning and I will be with you then.
I shall be gone by then.
I'll catch you up.
I hope you can. (Adapted from Luke 9:50-61)

As children of God, Jesus wants our total commitment. He said 'no one who puts his hand to the plough and looks back is fit for service in the Kingdom of God' (Luke 9:62). If that is what he wants, then I have a burning question that needs answering before I set out to follow him. And that question is 'Jesus, where does following you take me? What about eternal life?' We will find his answer in the next chapter.

CHAPTER TEN

SUCCESS – GAINING THE PRIZE

No one who puts a hand to the plough and looks back is fit for service in the kingdom of God. (Luke 9:62)

It was party time, and what a party it was. It was the sort of party held after passing an exam, made all the sweeter because it was a triumph after an initial failure. The mission of the twelve had flopped, but Jesus wasted no time. He got together a second mission, six times larger than the first. He commissioned seventy-two and sent them out in pairs.

Jesus' instructions to the seventy-two are very similar to the instructions that he had previously given to the twelve. But this time he spelt it out with more definition. First he identified their situation. They were as sheep among wolves (Luke 10:3). They were vulnerable, so it was imperative that they remained in pairs. As they walked the journey together, there would be times when one or the other might become disheartened so that, in their vulnerability, they would need each other. With that background in mind, Jesus gave the following instructions that would help them as they journeyed from village to village:

Rule one: don't take purse, bag or sandals (Luke 10:4). This was the same instruction as before. There would be nothing they possessed that would enable them to reap any kind of harvest for the kingdom of heaven. They were entirely dependent on God through Jesus.

Rule two: don't greet anyone on the road (Luke 10:4). In other words, don't get distracted by anything. They had a mission to achieve and that had to be foremost in their minds.

Rule three: where you stay, say 'peace to this house' (Luke 10:5). Giving peace was like giving them a pair of shoes. When people entered a house they left their shoes at the entrance. If the seventy-two were accepted, their peace remained in the house. If they were not accepted, they would find their peace by the door with the shoes as they departed. In other words, the peace that Jesus gave never left them whatever the circumstances.

Rule four: stay where you are (Luke 10:7). If they had found a welcome, they were to stay with it and not try to find somewhere which might look better or more important.

Would they succeed where the twelve had failed? I don't think that Jesus had any doubt, because they had learnt much from their failure. In the event, their mission was a complete success. The seventy-two returned with joy. Chapter ten contains one of those few moments in the gospel where there is sheer joy, the joy that comes from something well done. They were in heaven. This is where Jesus had taken them. 'He who listens to you, will listen to me,' (Luke 10:16), Jesus had told them before they set out, and they had listened alright! They had preached about the kingdom of heaven and healed the sick. They had put their hands to the plough and had not looked back.

Eternal life

Perhaps we can imagine that we joined the party with the seventy-two. I am particularly keen to be there because I want to find Jesus and ask him my question about eternal life. It doesn't take long for the opportunity to arrive because the seventy-two are all exhausted after their mission. So contentedly they begin to sprawl out, and my moment has come. Feeling a bit awkward, I drew close to Jesus.

Jesus, you said that you wanted my total commitment.
Yes.
That once I've started, it's like putting my hand on a plough and not looking back.
Are you going to get to the point?
Where does following you take me? What do I have to do to get eternal life?

Anxiously I blurted it out, hoping that he wouldn't dismiss me from his presence with a holy flea in my ear. He thought for a while before he replied:

You might like to think of eternal life as a prize.
OK. How do I win the prize?
Perhaps it might help if I told you a couple of stories. There are five people in these stories. Some won the prize but others didn't.
Will these stories help me to understand?
Yes, but you also might bear in mind the rules that helped guide the seventy-two in their mission.
What, the ones about not taking bag, purse and sandals and not stopping on the road?
That's right. But be warned – it might not be that straightforward.
OK – what's the first story?

The story of the Good Samaritan

The expert of the law

So Jesus began.

'The first story started with someone who asked the same question. An expert of the law stood up to test me.

"Teacher," he asked, "what must I do to inherit eternal life?"
I replied, "what is written in the law? How do you read it?"
He answered, "love the Lord your God with all your heart, and with all your soul, and with all your mind, and love your neighbour as yourself".
I said, "do this and you will live."'
(Adapted from Luke 10:25-27)

So that's the way to get the prize of eternal life, is it? Keep what amounts to the ten commandments, and the prize is ours. Yes?
That is certainly one way of getting the prize.
So the lawyer was right?
Well, not exactly.
But you told him that he was OK.
What I told him, if you remember, was to keep the law and he would live. Listen.

So I closed my mouth as he explained. 'The expert of the law took his purse, bag and sandals – which, to him, was the law. The law would entitle him to inherit eternal life. He had the law. He knew the law. He possessed the law. The law, he thought, justified him before God. He was deluded because he thought that he was capable of total obedience to the law and commandments. No one, not even him, could honestly say to have loved God and loved his neighbour all the time. Sometimes, maybe – but not all the time. The lesson from this is that no one, then or now, is capable of justifying themselves before God through the law.'

The priest

Jesus went on with the story. 'The expert of the law saw that he was in a bit of a hole, so he asked, 'and who is my neighbour?' So I told them a story of a man going down from Jerusalem to Jericho, when he fell into the hands of robbers. They stripped him of his clothes, beat him and went away, leaving him half dead. A priest happened to be going down the same road, and when he saw the man he passed by on the other side. In the same way, a Levite, also passed by on the other side.' (Adapted from Luke 10:25-27)

> So you would think that the priest would have got the prize...
> Yes, you would think so, wouldn't you?
> Well, he didn't greet anybody on the road.
> No, he rushed by and left the poor man there bleeding,
> And isn't there something in God's law that says that a priest would be defiled if he came into contact with someone's blood?
> Listen, no way was that priest fit for the prize.
> Yes, but he only did what he was meant to do, wasn't he?

He motioned me to calm down. 'This priest was doing what many do. He used law as an excuse, so that he didn't have to show common humanity. He justified himself - but God hated what he did. It is the sort of self-righteousness that causes deep distress in the workplace and within families. Worst of all, it crops up in church - which is why I have used this priest as an example'.

The Samaritan

Then Jesus finished the story. 'But a Samaritan, as he travelled, came where the man was, and when he saw him, he took pity on him. He went to him and bandaged his wounds, pouring on oil and wine. Then he put the man on his own donkey, bought him to an inn and took care of him. The next day he took out two silver coins and gave them to the innkeeper. 'Look after him,' he said, 'and when I return, I will reimburse you.' (Adapted from Luke 10:33-35)

> Well the Samaritan greeted someone on the road, didn't he?
> Yes. He greeted someone on the road who badly needed his help.
> But what about the fact that he was carrying bag, purse and sandals?
> This Samaritan was prepared to use his own resources to deal with the crisis before him.
> He must have been unpopular with the other Samaritans travelling with him.
> Yes - particularly if the injured man turned out to be a Jew!

I knew that was no small thing. Samaritans and Jews *hated* each other. However, as Jesus spoke I was beginning to realise that application of the rules wasn't quite as straightforward as it seemed at first.

Jesus went on to explain. The Samaritan did not rely on Law to justify himself before God, nor did he interpret the rules in a single-minded manner, as many do in all walks of life. This was a man who had the freedom within himself to use common sense, courtesy and love for others in every situation and to complete the task that he saw as important. He was a good neighbour, the best kind of neighbour. This neighbour was full of grace - that is, the favour of unearned love. This Samaritan was the sort of man we would all love to have next door.

> You have your answer. Which one do you think will get the prize of eternal life?
> The Samaritan, of course.
> Be like him then. Are you ready for the next story?

The story of Martha and Mary

So Jesus told his second story. 'I was with my disciples when we came to a village where a woman named Martha opened her home to us. She had a sister called Mary, who sat at my feet listening while I spoke. But Martha was distracted by all the preparations that had to be made. She came to me and said 'Lord, don't you care that my sister has left me to do all the work by myself? Tell her to help me!' I answered 'Martha, Martha, you are worried and upset about many things, but only one thing is needed. Mary has chosen what is better and it will not be taken away from her'. (Adapted from Luke 10:38-41)

> I can relate to Martha.
> Yes, we all know and love someone very much like her.
> What was her problem then?
> Her problem was that, unlike the Samaritan, she lost her peace.

He bent his head down, remembering.

'You see, Martha was amongst wolves - hungry wolves! How many were going to be sitting around the table that night? Would it be fifteen or sixteen of us? But Martha was capable. Nothing could beat her. Her purse, bag and sandals were her sheer determination to prepare that dinner. How we would all praise her for it afterwards!

'Then things started to go wrong - irritating things. She knew that it would be alright if she had a bit more help in the kitchen but she was on her own, with it all to do... and, well, inevitably she lost her peace of mind. Then...wham! She exploded!'

He flung his arms over his head in mock terror but actually he was grinning from ear to ear. We both bellowed with laughter but then Jesus quickly became serious again.

'You will find out more about Martha from John's gospel, and see that this troubled and searching soul would get the prize of eternal life - but right then her life was anything but eternal. There are so many who have lost their peace - or maybe never found it.'

Then he changed the subject to Martha's sister.

> And what about Mary? What do you think of her?
> She got it right.
> Yes, she was just being herself.

Carrying no bag, purse or sandals.
She greeted no one 'on the road' – she let nothing distract her, and she was completely at peace. No one could move Mary from her spot on the floor in front of me.
She definitely got it right then.

But Jesus wanted to make sure that I had understood about Mary.
'Listen,' he said, 'Mary knew that she was among wolves. They were in the kitchen in the form of her angry sister. She knew that there would be a massive fall-out with her sister before long. Yet she held onto her peace. Ever since we arrived in her house, she had felt a peace that wouldn't be taken away from her'.
He had one more point to make and he was determined that I heard it.
'Nothing distracted Mary from where she was. She didn't move, no matter how unfair that was to her sister. Sitting in her front room, listening to what I had to say, was an experience that would never happen again. Mary held onto her faith at a difficult moment - she chose something better and won the prize. In the same way, these moments will happen in your life and you should never let them pass - no matter what'.

Two on the road

The lesson was over and I reflected on the conversation. I looked at Mary and the Samaritan and saw them as one of the pairs sent out with the seventy-two commissioned by Jesus to bring the kingdom of God to their community. The pairing of these two people was a triumph – an absolute success. There was faith-filled Mary, who listened intently to everything that Jesus had said. There was the grace-filled Samaritan, who was prepared to do what was needed, even if that meant risking his reputation and life. Through their God-given qualities, they had won the prize. Eternal life was theirs. It is these qualities that are needed in each one of us if we are to do the same.

We need to understand, with the faith of Mary, that we are helpless and dependant on Jesus for any claim to eternal life. At the same time we need to have the grace of the Samaritan, who was prepared to use whatever resources were at his disposal to achieve any task that God set before him. However, not all of us possess full measures of faith and grace. Some of us are more like faith-filled Mary, whereas others are more like the grace-filled Samaritan. We need other people, particularly those who possess those qualities that we don't have. That is why Jesus sent the seventy-two out in pairs.

These two, Mary and the Samaritan, were amongst those who Jesus met as he set his face resolutely for Jerusalem. They would not have known what was in store for them as they followed Jesus but they had met someone very special. From Jesus came the knowledge that theirs was the kingdom of heaven and the prize of eternal life.

CHAPTER ELEVEN

OUR FATHER

When you pray, say 'Father...' (Luke 11:2)

My early Christian life was spent in a very large and influential church. The teaching that we received in that church was second to none. Later I had to move away from my 'Christian birthplace' but the words of my old mentor stayed with me: 'John, wherever you go, your church will not grow unless it prays together'.

Much water has gone under the bridge since then, but my mentor's words have always stayed with me. My church is now in a faith school in a growing residential area. Recently the church council took the decision that the church must pray together. Since that decision was taken, our church has grown and continues to grow. It is difficult to know exactly why. I don't think that we are doing anything very different except one thing – communicating with God. Praying together.

Teach us to pray

Joy, happiness, and gladness were everywhere. The seventy-two had returned and everybody was smiling. They were looking forward to the challenges ahead, for they were following the Christ of God on his way to Jerusalem. As they celebrated at the home of Martha and Mary (hopefully Martha had got over her frustration), only Jesus was fully aware of what lay ahead. But for now, his disciples were happy and so was he.

So imagine Jesus' delight when one of the disciples observed how dependent he was on prayer. That disciple realised that the success of the seventy-two must have had something to do with those hours that Jesus spent on his own communicating with God. He wanted to do that himself, so he approached Jesus with a request; 'Lord, teach us to pray' (Luke 11:1). What resulted from this request was the greatest prayer ever given to mankind. The Lord's Prayer suffices for every moment and every situation of the day.

> Lord, give us what we need – our daily bread.
> Forgive us when we get it wrong.
> Protect us when we come up against it.
> (Adapted from Luke 11:1-2)

These are the essential ingredients of the prayer handed down to us and it was born out of the needs of those following Jesus to his destiny at Jerusalem.

Give us our daily bread

How many times have I said the words 'give us this day our daily bread'? What possible right have I got to ask God, the creator of the universe, to look after my daily needs? The answer is clear – I have absolutely no rights at all. Such a request would most certainly be rightfully condemned, had not Jesus himself told us to make it. He effectively gave us permission to make this impertinent approach to God.

But does God really take any notice? I am convinced that this was on the disciple's minds when they heard Jesus teaching them this part of the prayer. Because of this unspoken question in the minds of the disciples, Jesus said to them:

> Which of you fathers, if your son asks for a fish will give him a snake... If you then who are evil know how to give good gifts to your children, how much more will your Father in heaven give the Holy Spirit to those who ask him.
> (Adapted from Luke 11:11-13)

In a strange sort of way, I have found this promise to be a bit confusing. Jesus assures us that God will answer our needs. Yet I am sure that I am not alone when I say that at times I have severely doubted this promise.

Some years ago my mother was in hospital, soon to die. Someone very close was suffering from an eating disorder. A colleague's husband had been sent to prison. And the fridge had broken down. This was followed in succession by the breakdown of the boiler and then the oven. Furthermore, I was due to go into hospital for a minor operation, and the hospital had screwed up the arrangements and...well do forgive me, God, when I say that this all looks very snake-like to me!

I am sure most of us can relate to times when life is like this. Then I read this verse, which effectively says, 'don't worry. I have it under control. I, your God, have only good gifts to give you. Look - here is my Holy Spirit....' (Adapted from Luke 11:13)

> Err...thanks God...very much - but I'm not sure that it's your Holy Spirit that I want right now. I really need something a bit more concrete, like money or food or a break from the misery that is going on all around me.
> WHAT I REALLY WANT IS...!

So I came to look at the parable that follows the Lord's Prayer, and realised that I had got it the wrong way round. The request, 'give us this day our daily bread' is not first and foremost about us. Primarily it's about God helping me to provide others with what they need and provision for my needs are to follow. The vital word in the Lord's Prayer is 'us' – give *us* this day our daily bread.

The parable or story that follows is about a man who knocks on the door of a neighbour at midnight with the news that he has received an unexpected visitor but has nothing to give him to eat. The neighbour is understandably far from happy about being disturbed and objects to getting up out of bed. However, he eventually relents because the man won't give up knocking on his door.

Now just suppose we have got home from a hard day at work. We slump down on the sofa and turn on the television and put our feet up. Then a thought comes to mind that we ought to ring someone who needs our support but we are very tired. So let us suppose that the man in Jesus' story (the one knocking on the door) represents our mind, and his reluctant neighbour is our body. God the Holy Spirit comes to our mind with a thought:

Holy Spirit: Mind!
Mind: What?
Holy Spirit: Wake up.
Mind: What do you want?
Holy Spirit: Ring Andy.
Mind: Why?

Holy Spirit: You know why. He lost his job yesterday.

Mind: But it's late!

Holy Spirit: No it's not. Its only 9 o'clock.

Mind: But I can't do it myself. I haven't got the resources.

Holy Spirit: I know you haven't. You'll need to get body up.

Mind: But body's asleep.

Holy Spirit: Wake him up then!

Mind: He won't like it...

Holy Spirit: Just wake him up

Mind: Oh, alright. Body!

Body: ...errmm...

Mind: Body!

Body: Go away!

Mind: You've got to get up.

Body: I said GO AWAY!

Mind: We have to make a phone call.

Body: Tomorrow.

Mind: No...now!

Body: I'm tired now!

Mind: Get up.

Body: I have worked so hard all day

Mind: Get up!

Body: ALL DAY I have worked SO HARD

Mind: Get up!

Body: Oh for goodness sake!

Mind: Get up.

Body: Okay..okay...okay. Get this over with and then perhaps I can have a bit of peace.

Mind and body: Andy, is that you? I heard you lost your job. I'm so sorry mate...

(Adapted from Luke 11:5-8)

Looking at it this way, the gift of the Holy Spirit becomes very relevant. When we are faced with the needs of others, we can become very aware of our emptiness and that our cupboard is bare. What we need more than anything else is the gift of God's Holy Spirit to enliven the mind and enable the body. Give us what we need; breathe your Holy Spirit into us so that we can provide for each other. When we understand this we can begin to understand Jesus' promise that follows:

Ask and it will be given to you; seek and you will find; knock and the door will be opened to you. (Luke 11:9)

Jesus' promise is not to just to ask for money or to get that job. I don't think that Jesus wants us to think of it just this way. Jesus said that we are to knock on God's door for whoever is in need and the door will be open. Jesus promises that God gives only good gifts if we do this. Give *us* this day our daily bread. Please give my neighbour his daily bread. Give me the Holy Spirit so that this might happen. This is the first essential need for all journeys of life and it was the first essential need for their journey to Jerusalem.

Forgive us our sins

Conversely, the request 'forgive us our sins' is all about us. If the Holy Spirit is essential in giving us our daily bread, then it plays just as important a part in the request to forgive our sins. Paul sums it up well:

I do not understand what I do. For what I want to do, I do not do, but what I hate, I do (Romans 7:15)

I think Paul had a wry smile on his face as he wrote this because it completely describes our human behaviour. There is a battle going on in each one of us and the problem is that we are apt to lose most of the fights.

The disciples must have felt strong as they set out for Jerusalem with the Christ of God at their head; yet each of them would be overtaken by something stronger. A day was soon coming when, much against their will, they would all desert Jesus. Like the disciples, we too might feel strong and capable - yet there will come a time when we will come up against something that we cannot overcome. It is as if something stronger has taken over and we are no longer in control. We do what we don't want to do. We need the Holy Spirit of God to sweep our bodies clean and to bring us back to what we want to be. We need the Holy Spirit now and continuously.

Forgive us our sins – give us your Holy Spirit. Being given forgiveness is a process of clearing out, sweeping clean and emptying the garbage afflicting our lives. This is followed by filling, refurnishing and starting again. However, Jesus makes it clear that it is absolutely essential that this process of emptying and filling be continuous. If it is not continuous, then will find ourselves in greater difficulties than before.

An example of what this means is happening in my own life right now. This is shared by men and women of a certain age like me. My life has always been busy, but recently I retired. The daily routine of commuting to London, of spending my life looking at a screen interspersed with office banter suddenly came to an end. However it was absolutely essential that, after retirement, I re-filled my life. I had to start again with something different. The idea of doing nothing, whilst initially attractive, could not remain. If I stayed idle, my life would be overtaken by something else, something infinitely worse. Boredom would take over, which in turn would breed resentment, or criticism, or condemnation, self-righteousness, or pride. The danger was that I would become a modern day Pharisee – grumpily disaffected as my life became more and more irrelevant.

Forgive us our sins – fill us with your Holy Spirit ... and keep filling us. Above all don't stop filling us. This is for all people of all ages; for if this doesn't happen we will fall into temptation.

Lead us not into temptation

Luke shows two specific areas where we should be most wary and need the most protection. These two temptations will ransack our lives if they are allowed to take hold. They are represented by two groups of people – the Pharisees and the teachers of the law.

The Pharisees

The Pharisees were devoted to appearances. When I was a very young boy of nine or ten, I was in church listening to a sermon. At that age most of the sermons that I heard meant absolutely nothing and would be judged solely on their length. Yet this one stuck in my mind. The man preaching the sermon produced two apparently identical white pocket handkerchiefs, both neatly folded. When they were unfolded, one of the handkerchiefs was beautifully white throughout, whereas the other had a big black stain within. From that moment on, I realised that this is how some people are. This is how Pharisees are.

Jesus was invited to a Pharisee's house for something to eat, only to be criticised for not washing before the meal (Luke 11:37-38). What a miserable experience that must have been! His hosts outwardly displayed hospitality yet inwardly they were harbouring criticism. They were just like the black stain on the inside of the neatly folded white handkerchief. Jesus' parting word to them must have stung. They were like dirty cups - only clean on the outside. They made their financial offerings yet neglected love and justice. They were utterly self-indulgent. Look at me on the top table! Look at me rubbing shoulders with the great and good!

Nothing indicates to me that God has a problem with appearance – he likes us to look good. But it seems clear from stories in the bible that God has a deep, deep loathing of appearances. Look at those two words. They are so similar.

APPEARANCE
APPEARANCES

What is the difference? The difference is an 'S' – a snake that will produce a monster devoted to appearance which therefore cannot be trusted. Lead us not into temptation. Protect us from being like the Pharisees.

The teachers of the law

The teachers of the law ransacked lives. They burdened people with an endless succession of rules. Today it is the same. The rules may be different but the constant stream of laws, regulations and political correctness equally ransacks the spirit of people today. Our 'teachers of the law', however, are difficult to identify because effectively we have brought on ourselves a culture of dependence on laws and rules, which in turn separates us from taking responsibility for both ourselves and others.

We burden both parents and teachers with rules. We suffer from procedures to combat the rising compensation culture, which is forever demanding an unobtainable, risk-free environment. We are increasingly unable to say what we believe should it offend the 'isms' of race, sex or age. Rules are introduced in an effort to stamp out unfairness yet often serve to produce unfairness in other directions.

I understand the necessity of having laws and rules to guide us in living well together. Rules are necessary to help us, particularly when we live crowded on top of each other. I also understand the need for rules when it comes to self-discipline. But when rules grow into obsession they squash freedom, stultify all imagination, and disable any ability to make decisions through fear of making mistakes. Lead us not into temptation. Don't let us burden others with our rules.

Let this be our prayer today and on our journey through life:

> Our Father, give us what you have promised, give us your kingdom. Give us what we need for others and then for ourselves. Sweep out sin within us and anything that separates us from you and then fill us with your Holy Spirit again and again. And don't let us be fooled into thinking that God thinks that appearances are important or spend our time burdening others with our rules.

CHAPTER TWELVE

TRAMPLING

But seek his kingdom and these things will be given to you as well
(Luke 12:31)

Feet! Feet were everywhere. Kicking, pushing, stamping and trampling...yes, trampling, and not caring who they trampled on. There were thousands of feet, and of course there were twice as many feet as there were people gathered around Jesus. It was becoming a familiar sight but they all wanted to get close and hear what he had to say. They all wanted to get within range because they wanted answers.

Jesus told his disciples to take care not to get trampled. He wasn't referring to thousands of feet in a crowd but to something more dangerous still. Be on your guard against the Pharisees who will trample on you. Be on your guard against those who use their positions of authority to squash the freedom out of you. And, continued Jesus, be on your guard against those who whisper behind your back.

Today it's called the 'rat race' and it affects not just the workplace. The rat race is a scramble for the top spot, wherever that might be. It demands that we think ahead, gain the upper ground and trample on anyone else that tries to get there as well. This results in a culture of worry, particularly worry about the future and how we will manage. But Jesus has a message for us. It is a key message in chapter twelve to all those who feel trampled over and unable to fulfil their potential. This is it,

> *Seek his kingdom, and these things will be given to you as well*
> *(Luke 12:31)*

God is for today. Worry is about tomorrow. Forget today and we will overlook God. It is a vicious spiral and it is why worriers struggle with God. There are three types of worriers that come out of Luke chapter twelve. There are sparrows, rich fools and ravens. Let us see how we might fit with any of these.

Sparrows

Sparrows feel worthless. They feel worthless to others, worthless to God and worthless to themselves. Jesus said, 'are not five sparrows sold for two pennies?' in Luke 12:16.

Who are today's sparrows? Anybody who is affected by the trampling effects of bullying or abuse; those who have been put down so many times that they find if hard to defend themselves. Sparrows put up with abuse and would do anything for a quiet life.

Sparrows worry about all sorts of things. Some worry about money and some worry about what to wear. Some worry about saying the right thing. Some worry about their reputation, some worry about illness and some worry about how long they are going to live. It is not easy to own to being a sparrow because we like to appear to be strong even when deep down we are anything but strong. Strip away the veneer and we hear people constantly putting themselves down, claiming that they are somehow not good enough. They are afraid of a new challenge, thinking that they haven't got the right qualifications or the right experience. Their confidence is shot and they find themselves no better than sparrows in a world full of aspiring vultures. But look at Luke chapter twelve and see that Jesus came into the world for the sparrows.

> *Not (one sparrow) is forgotten by God...Don't be afraid; you are worth more than many sparrows. (Luke 12:6-7)*

Sparrows are in good company. 'Don't be afraid!' were the words used by the angel to Mary, to the shepherds in the field, and to old Zachariah. It was, we will see, the words that Jesus used to his disciples when he appeared to them after his resurrection. Recently I used the same words to a man who was worrying about a letter that he had in his hand from his employer. It summoned him to a meeting because, they maintained, he wasn't up to his job. He was frightened about his future. But Jesus says to all worriers 'seek the kingdom of heaven and these things will be given to you as well'.

It might be that today might not be the best day of our lives to seek the kingdom of heaven. We might be too busy or too distracted - but what

Jesus is asking us to do is very un-sparrowlike. He tells us to seek the kingdom of heaven. To do this we have to stop being like sparrows and put our trust in God. If we are able to that, then the promise of Jesus is that he will take care of those things that worry us. 'Seek first the kingdom of heaven and all these things (whose lack worries us) will be given to you as well'.

Leaving sparrows for the moment, let us look at another type of person who was worried about the future. This was the rich fool.

The rich fool

If we don't like to admit that we are sparrows, then we equally don't like to own up to behaving like rich fools. Rich fools are also worriers and Jesus had a warning for them, which he told in a parable. You can find the story in Luke twelve. Here is another version of the story. The following is entirely fictitious but it might bear out some home truths in our lives.

Obituary: Francis Oliver Oswald Loghead

Francis Loghead, known as Frank to his friends, was born on 30 February 1944. He was educated at St Ashtrays's College, Dumpon. School reports about him were mixed, although it was observed by the headmaste in a report to his parents that young Frank had a tendency to want to play around the garbage area. On leaving school, he found his first job with the waste disposal department of the local council and he realised that he had found his vocation in life. It wasn't long before he formed his own company, Loghead Disposals Ltd. The company went from strength to strength but his fortune was made in what became nicknamed 'the intelligent dustbin'. This was a household device that could separate bio-degradable waste from other waste. With huge national demand and a patent to protect the product, Loghead Disposals became one of the largest waste disposal companies in the country, with Loghead himself becoming a millionaire several times over.

Francis Loghead had a passion for dustbins. His collection of dustbins became the largest in the world, In later years he determined to house his collection under one roof. So he built a large museum in his 100 acre country estate. His dearest wish was to sit back and enjoy his dustbin collection in retirement. Regrettably, only months after completing the project, Frank Loghead died. It was subsequently found that the new museum contravened planning regulations and it had to be demolished. The collection of dustbins was sold off for scrap.

Francis Loghead was married five times and is survived by all his ex-wives. His fifth wife gave a fitting epitaph at his funeral, saying, 'rubbish was his life'
(Adapted from Luke 12:13-21)

As I see it, neither Francis Loghead nor the rich fool in Jesus' parable did much that was very wrong, humanly speaking. However, the point of Jesus' parable was to tell us about this sort of worrier. He wouldn't have even thought of himself as a worrier but rather that he was providing for himself. He was on top of things - or so he thought.

What the worried fool was doing was putting a wall around him so that he could keep God out. He had no concern for God and he probably felt that God had no concern for him either. He had eyes only for himself and seeking the kingdom of heaven was furthest from his mind. A rich fool's prayer might be coined like this:

Our Father
Give me the kingdom and all good things
Give me what is rightfully mine
And give me somewhere to put it. Amen

Ravens

We come to the third type of worrier – the raven.

Consider the ravens: They do not sow or reap, they have no storeroom or barn; yet God feeds them. And how much more valuable you are than birds! Who of you by worrying can add a single hour to your life? Since you cannot do this very little thing, why do you worry about the rest? (Luke 12:24-26)

The raven was apparently considered cursed by the religious leaders of the day and so the raven represents those who feel cursed. 'Ravens' in the world feel just as trampled on as 'sparrows' and they worry just as much. Who are the ravens? Amongst 'the cursed' are women who think that they are fat when they are really quite slim. There are men who are convinced that they deeply unattractive. There are people who feel accident-prone, or like the world somehow has it in for them. Feeling cursed comes in many forms and for a variety of different reasons. It may be because of sexuality, or an obsession, or because of a relationship breakdown. Feeling cursed is a terrible form of trampling, and can be self-inflicted. The advice that Jesus gives to all who feel cursed is the same. Seek his kingdom and these things will be given to you as well.

A few years ago I found that God cared for me when I was going through an intense 'ravenlike' experience. I was at the lowest ebb of my life, at a time when I was on my own and feeling utterly cut off from all - bar a very few. I felt so vulnerable that I found myself checking every move with God, such was my need of him. I was literally seeking his kingdom day by day - not because I was good at understanding his teaching but because I had nowhere else to go. In the depths of my troubles, God showed himself to me in a quite remarkable way.

I walked each weekday from my tiny flat to the station to catch a train to work. The short walk took me through a rather beautiful churchyard. One sunny morning, as I was walking through the churchyard, a pure white dove flew down and landed on the path right in front of me. It was so close that I had to take care where I stepped for fear of treading on it as it weaved itself between my feet. I wouldn't have thought any more on it if it wasn't for the fact that it happened again in just the same way the following morning. This time there was a woman also walking in the churchyard. 'How remarkable!' she exclaimed as I picked my way carefully over the bird. On the third morning the dove was there again, nearby, perched on a headstone, looking at me as I passed. I never saw it again.

To those who are going through a 'ravenlike' experience at the moment, it is good to remind ourselves that we have actually met quite a few cursed ravens in Luke's gospel already. Perhaps we might remind ourselves of them

There was the prostitute who wiped Jesus' feet with ointment and her tears.
There was the mad man running naked among tombs.
There was a woman who was a social outcast because of an embarrassing illness.
There was Jairus whose beloved daughter was dying.
There was a cursed Samaritan who turned out to be the best neighbour anybody could have.
There was a widow who lived in Nain who had lost the will to live because her only son had died.
Not least there was Mary the mother of Jesus, pregnant and unmarried.

When we feel like ravens, we must remember that we are not alone.

Watching

'Seek the kingdom of God' is what Jesus commands to all sparrows, ravens and rich fools. We do this by being ready and watching out for God. This watching overcomes worry, overcomes inferiority and self indulgence. Seeking the kingdom of God brings us closer to God and, being closer to God, we become less like sparrows or ravens or rich fools. Seeking the kingdom of God reverses that downward spiral.

Some tend to think that watching is the prerogative of God. They talk about their guardian angels. 'Someone must have been watching over me,' is an expression that I sometimes hear. God does watch over us as a loving father watches over his children - he watched over me as I walked through that churchyard. But Jesus has watching the other way round.

> Be dressed ready for service and keep your lamps burning, like servants waiting for their master to return from a wedding banquet, so that when he comes and knocks they can immediately open the door for him. (Luke 12:35-36)

The type of 'watching' that Jesus refers to is set within a very loving relationship. It is the type of watching that a loving husband does for his wife. It is no accident that the servants were dressed and ready for their master's return from a wedding banquet. Their watching was set within the love of marriage. A husband listens for his wife's return if she has been out late, or is ready with the car to pick her up. This might equally apply to a parent listening for the return of one of their children. This is not watching with tapping fingers, ready to strike with the rolling pin the moment that the 'loved one' appears through the front door. This stems rather from a deep loving desire to know that your loved one is alright whilst, at the same time, wanting the best for them.

Jesus then extends the parable to tell us the unfortunate consequences of the times we don't watch for God. He tells us what might happen if the servant's watch extends into the small hours of the morning.

> *But suppose the servant says to himself 'My master is taking a long time in coming' and he begins to beat the other servants, both men and women, and to eat and drink and get drunk. (Luke 12:45)*

Why watch for God if he is not coming? Perhaps, after all, God does not exist! Jesus tells us that the consequence of not seeking the kingdom of God is that we trample on each other in a rat-race of self preservation. This is clearly evident today. Taking their eyes off God clearly appeals to many and the result is that sparrows, ravens and rich fools continue to abound.

But God does not enter the rat-race. He doesn't make himself bigger than everybody else and throw his weight around. Instead he gets down to the level of the sparrows and the ravens and makes himself small, so small that it is easy to think that he is not there - a mistake that many people make.

CHAPTER THIRTEEN

SMALL

What is the Kingdom of God like? ...It is like a mustard seed...
(Luke 13:18-19)

In church we sing a favourite children's song: 'my God is so big, so strong and so mighty, there's nothing that he cannot do'. If we think of God at all, we think of him as creator and that means he must be very big. Reaching back to the very beginning of this book, it was the size of God that caused my father problems. Both John the Baptist and Simon Peter had problems with Jesus when they realised who he was because Jesus was not in the same league as them. Yet in chapter thirteen Jesus shows us God in a completely different light. He shows us God as small – very small.

> Jesus, what is the Kingdom of God like?
> It is like a mustard seed – that is very small (Luke 13:19)
> Jesus, what is the Kingdom of God like?
> It is like yeast – that is even smaller (Luke 13:21)
> Jesus, how do I enter the Kingdom of God?
> Through a door - a very narrow door (Luke 13:24)

The majesty of God is not just that he can be very big but also that he can be very small. He made himself small so that he could reach out to tiny specks like us within his creation. The smallness of God enables him to reach out everywhere and go anywhere. The magnificence of God is that he made himself small, as small as us, as small as specks, equivalent to the size of a mustard seed or a tiny yeast. Perhaps once in a while we might change the words of that children's song and sing 'My God is so small, so teeny, so tiny, there's nowhere that he cannot go'.

God made himself accessible to us through Jesus. He made himself small but, because of this, it is very easy to miss him - and many do.

Despair

Jesus was now well and truly on his way. He was walking towards his destination at Jerusalem. He went through towns and villages and on the way people met him and others followed him.

It was a hard journey for him, as he was not well received by some. 'Leave this place and go somewhere else,' (Luke 13:31) some religious leaders said to him. They feared the trouble he might bring to them. So Jesus left them. He was going anyway. He had to go and nothing would stop him. But then suddenly, on the road ahead of them, he stopped and cried out in despair as if he had fallen under a great weight, like the weight of the cross that he was soon to carry.

> *Jerusalem, Jerusalem, you who kill the prophets and stone those sent to you, how often I have longed to gather your children together, as a hen gathers her chicks under her wings, and you were not willing. (Luke 13:34)*

What caused such anguish? Was it being told by religious leaders to move on? This would be very hurtful, but I don't think this was the main cause of his despair. No, I think it was because they, the people and the religious leaders, simply couldn't understand. He, the Impossible, had made himself small for us – too small for many. He wanted to gather them together as chicks but they thought themselves too big. They were not willing to admit that they were small.

There are two very similar stories either side of this cry of despair, and we will find the cause of his anguish in these stories.

Seeing the sky

The first of these stories is about a crippled woman. She was bent over and was unable to straighten up. Jesus described her as 'kept bound for eighteen years,' (Luke 13:16). So Jesus healed her. He set her free but, incredibly, he was criticised by the church leaders for having healed her on the Sabbath. Perhaps we can find ourselves in the story of this very small bent woman.

> Have you thought how it would be
> Bent to the ground and unable to see

Unable to see a smiling face
Or a look of love in any place
Bound for years - please hear my cry
I'm bent to the ground, not seeing the sky

I've strayed many times over the years
Recalling those times with eyes of tears
Gripped by habits of sins that I do
Longing to be free – well wouldn't you?
But I cannot break free however I try
Still bent to the ground, not seeing the sky

I have faith in one who can set me free
I have faith in him but others can't see
I have come to him but they bind him with rules
Crippled by rules adhered to by fools
I listen to them and breathe a great sigh
Bent to the ground, not seeing the sky

I have faith in him who I cannot see
Who touches my infirmity
Releasing me from sin and pain
And every single mark and stain
He's my God and I'll tell you why
I'm not bent to the ground but see the sky

No rules can bind this Christ of God
No sin can overcome his word
He came to the world from glory above
He came with everlasting love
I'm upright now and ready to fly
Not bent to the ground but seeing the sky
(Adapted from Luke 13:10-17)

Jesus set the crippled woman free from the tyranny that bound her. He freed her from those who sought to keep her bound. Now she could see the sky again. I would have loved to have been there and seen the joy in that woman's face as she straightened up for the first time. I would have loved to have seen the humiliation suffered by Jesus' opponents for their stupidity. I would have loved to have joined with delight with those others who acknowledged the wonderful things that he was doing.

Oedema

I have stretched into chapter fourteen for the second of these stories around Jesus' anguish because it bears a lot of similarity to the first story of the crippled woman. Again it was the Sabbath, and this time Jesus was in the house of a prominent religious leader when a man who was bloated and swollen stood before him, suffering from oedema (Luke 14:1-6). The Oxford English Dictionary describes the condition as 'an excess of watery fluid in the cavities or tissues of the body'. This is oedema, or dropsy as it was commonly known.

Perhaps those who loved to criticise Jesus recalled the humiliation that the leader of the church had suffered over the incident of the bent woman. Nobody said anything this time. No verbalised objections – just looking to see what would happen. But Jesus was not fazed by this. He knew their legalistic thoughts and healed the man anyway.

They hadn't learned anything. They had made no progress. Instead they stuck obdurately to their rules, even at the expense of these small people – one bent double and the other miserably swollen. Therein lies the reason for Jesus' anguish on the road. It is the same anguish that he would have for us today. 'I have longed to gather you together, but you would not listen,'

Bent to the ground

Can we relate this to our circumstances today? The culture and civilisation in Jesus' time was very different to how ours is. Even by the standards of the first century AD, central Palestine was a backwater, impoverished by an occupying force of the Roman Empire. They would have known what it was like to live lives bent to the ground. Yet today, with our comparative wealth, our welfare state and our National Health Service, many still live bent to the ground.

It's not a Roman army that has invaded to occupy us, but we have been invaded by other 'armies' that bend us to the ground. There is the weekly trial of making ends meet while we see others using their positions of authority to line their own pockets. We cry 'foul' as job opportunities grow scarcer and wages are cut - for those fortunate enough to have jobs. I am writing this during an economic crash, realising that it is a repeat of all that we went through only a few years ago. We seem to have learned nothing and instead have stuck obdurately to the mistakes of the past and, bent to the ground, many cry out in despair just as Jesus cried out in despair.

The cry goes out from some that we have no need for God - that it is time to free ourselves from irrelevant religion - but in our bid to be free, we find ourselves gripped by other occupying forces. It seems that, like the Pharisees of old, the more we move away from God the creator, the more we become occupied by the gods of greed, rules and lack.

Jesus came to save us from the tyranny that bends our backs to the ground. 'I have longed to gather you together – please listen'.

Repent

What did Jesus want to tell us in his anguish? His answer is recorded in chapter thirteen:

Unless you repent, you too will all perish (Luke 13:3)

The word 'repent' is a word that many tend to shun. It brings to me images of ranting preachers spilling out their own brand of condemnation. But Jesus uses the word 'repent', so perhaps we need to look at the word again. It might help if we looked at the word 'repent' as a reality check. When the rulers of the church had so stupidly objected to Jesus healing the bent-over woman on the Sabbath, they lost all sense of reality. If they were to overcome their obduracy, they would have to come to their senses and realise the idiocy of what they were standing for. What they needed was a complete change of hearts and minds. This is what repentance is.

In the same way, it does no harm for any of us from time to time to take a reality check and remind ourselves just who we are. We are small – very small. Beside God we are specks – very small specks. Through repentance, we might see the pointlessness of shackling ourselves and others with greed. Through repentance, we might see the occupying forces of fear and deprivation that torment our lives. Through the reality check of repentance we might see the anguish we cause to God who doesn't want us to be this way. Repentance is an acknowledgement that we don't want to go on the way we are any more. Repentance is therefore not something to be avoided but rather it is something to be welcomed. This is listening to Jesus as he calls us to himself.

The fig tree

To help us to further understand repentance, Luke records that Jesus told a parable about a fig tree he passed by that produced no fruit. A fig tree with no fruit is as useless as a pub with no beer. You might as well cut it down. Then a gardener comes along and pleads for the tree. 'Give me one year,' he asks, 'and I will tend it and love it. If it produces no fruit after that then it's for the chop!' (Adapted from Luke 13:6-9)

Many years ago I preached on the passage about the fig tree to a sparse congregation. My church was struggling. There was a lack of understanding of Jesus in that church. In my talk I asked the congregation to imagine Jesus passing by our church in the same way as he passed by the fig tree and I asked them to imagine what he would do if he found that our church bore no fruit. I pointed out that the evidence of what might result could be seen in the many deconsecrated churches littered all over towns and cities today - all of which had withered from the roots. Shocking as my message was, it seemed likely to have little effect as there were few to hear it!

But it did have an effect because I believe that God heard it. A very small hardcore group of Christians in the congregation faced up to the reality of our smallness and, in our repentance, we came together and stuck together. We even tried to pray together. We weren't very good at it, but we tried! Then we were joined by a wonderful young clergyman who became a lifelong friend both to me and others in that small little group. With his guidance and with the reality of our repentance the church began to bear fruit. It was only later that I came to realise just how close our church came to being shut down. I am no longer part of that church but it thrives to this day.

Jesus is our gardener, pleading for us where we produce no fruit, pleading for us where we shackle ourselves with other gods, pleading for us when we need to take a reality check. 'Give me a year while I tend to it, dig round it and fertilise it'. In other words, he is giving us all a chance but, at the same time, he doesn't guarantee what will happen next year. From this we might gather that if we continue as we are, then we too might be in for the chop.

The narrow door

So it seems that to enter the kingdom of heaven, we will have to take a reality check and recognise that we are small. That will be very difficult for any who are striving to be big or at least bigger than others. But God is quite the opposite, for he is prepared to make himself very small. Jesus says in the middle of the chapter

> *Someone asked him, 'Lord, are only a few people going to be saved?'* *He said to them, 'Make every effort to enter through the narrow door, because many, I tell you, will try to enter and will not be able to. Once the owner of the house gets up and closes the door, you will stand outside knocking and pleading,' 'Sir, open the door for us.' But he will answer, 'I don't know you or where you come from.' Then you will say, 'We ate and drank with you, and you taught in our streets.' But he will reply, 'I don't know you or where you come from.'* *(Luke 13:23-27)*

I have known about Jesus for many years and, as I read this gospel of Luke, I am finding Jesus to be increasingly fascinating. He is the person who I increasingly want to know. Therefore I would hate to think that he might shut the narrow door in my face and say 'I don't know you or where you have come from'. If you feel as I do about this, you will probably come to the same realisation, that there will be times when we, in our smallness, will need to take a reality check – and that might need to happen quite frequently.

But I also believe that every time he shuts the narrow door and says 'I don't know you,' he turns away in anguish – the same anguish that he cried with on the road to Jerusalem.

CHAPTER FOURTEEN

COST

And whoever does not carry their cross and follow me cannot be my disciple (Luke 14:27)

In 1881 a man called James Jezreel (aka James White) decided to build a huge tower in my home town. His intention was that it should be a truly impressive building to be used as the headquarters of his religious sect. The headquarters were to measure 124 feet on each side, and 120 feet high, constructed with eight soaring towers around a central circular assembly room which was to rise a height of 100 feet and be capped by a dome. The external walls were etched grandly with large trumpets and crossed swords. However, this project wasn't just about the tower, it was about a community, including a parade of shops also being constructed on the site fronting the main road. The cost was estimated at £25,000. This was to be a testimony to God - and probably to James Jezreel as well.

But then the scheme went wrong. James Jezreel took to drink and died. His young wife took over the building project, but the cost of the project got out of hand, which led to dissent among the sect. Building was brought to a halt, but not before the structure of the tower, together with the shops, was largely completed. Builders returned to the site a mere 24 years after the project's conception but this time with the intention of knocking the tower down. But even that didn't work, as the contractors went bust, leaving the walls, now at only half their original height and open for all to see. In the early 1960s the tower was finally demolished and the shops, which had been empty for years and formed the last remnant of the project, were finally pulled down in 2008.

I remember as a boy being fascinated by the Jezreel's Tower. I would ride on the top deck of the bus so that I could see over the perimeter wall and observe the ruined edifice with its trumpets and swords etched on the elevations. It looked a scary place, somewhere that I wouldn't want to enter, as if it held some sort of warning. This irrelevant and ridiculous building was no testimony to God.

Counting the cost

With the Jezreels Tower in mind, you might see how I relate to the following parable, which Jesus told toward the end of chapter fourteen of Luke's gospel:

> *Suppose one of you wants to build a tower. Won't you first sit down and estimate the cost to see if you have enough money to complete it? For if you lay the foundation and are not able to finish it, everyone who sees it will ridicule you, saying, 'This person began to build and wasn't able to finish.' (Luke 14:28-30)*

The message seems clear, - count the cost of what you are getting into before you get into it. Jesus backed it up by telling another parable with the same message, following hard after the parable of the tower. It's about a king who had second thoughts about going to war with another king, whose army was larger and more powerful. The king decided wisely that discretion was the part of valour and so sued for peace (Luke 14:31-32).

What is Jesus teaching us here with these stories? Is Jesus saying that we should not undertake anything unless we have effectively eliminated all risk? Lets face it, there is always risk in both building development and in war.

Underneath these stories there is a deeper point being made. I have known of building projects undertaken in faith without a perfect understanding of where all the money was coming from. I have known of personal decisions taken in faith without a true understanding of where it might lead. I think of a young missionary family I know who have taken the decision to live and work in Peru. Do they know where that decision will take them? I think of an ex-colleague who has recently taken the decision to go out on his own and become self employed. Does he know where this will lead? I think of nations going to war against the odds. Chartwell, the home of Winston Churchill, is not far from where I live. Every time I go there, I am reminded of the courageous decision that he and others took to pursue the war against Nazism in spite of the fact that the enemy seemed better prepared.

Looking at these stories, I believe Jesus is teaching that before undertaking any decision in our lives, we should make sure that our hearts are in it and that our feet are on the ground. Every project, particularly the more important ones, involves our whole being, head and heart, dwelling solidly within the undertaking, for the rest of what life offers. Just as importantly, the project must also remain solidly within the lives of those who support us in our undertaking. We may take wrong turnings, go up blind alleys and take wrong decisions, but that deep desire to complete whatever project is rooted in our hearts remains within us and within our support. Jesus said in chapter fourteen:

> And whoever does not carry their cross and follow me, cannot be my disciple. (Luke 14:27)

When we count the cost, we are counting money – but not just money. We are counting the cost of our commitment and the commitment of others. When we count the cost of following Jesus, we are carrying our cross.

Carrying the cross

Jesus was on his way to Jerusalem. Luke tells us that a large crowd was following him as he strode toward his destiny. He was thinking he had something that he had to tell them, something he had to get clear. Suddenly he turned round and faced them.

> If anyone comes to me and does not hate father and mother, wife and children, brothers and sisters – yes even life itself – such a person cannot be my disciple. (Luke 14:26-27)

Jesus was looking at them as he looks at us. Do we know what it means to follow Jesus? Do we understand what we are letting ourselves in for? Are we ready to carry our cross, whatever that might be? Because if we follow him, we will carry some form of cross. Following Jesus requires our total commitment and our absolute priority. This commitment is over family mother, father, wife, children. Are we ready for this? We cannot follow Jesus unless we are ready for this.

It doesn't seem much of a welcome, does it? There were many in that large crowd that were not ready to follow him and it is the same for us today. No wonder Jesus taught that the door to the kingdom was narrow. Following Jesus is not for those who follow the crowd, nor is it for the faint hearted. So before we decide to follow Jesus we must count the cost. We must understand for certain that following him is the deepest desire of our hearts. The cross that we will carry will be our destiny and will represent the greatest achievement of our lives because it is from God. But at times it will seem far from easy. Here are two examples, and in these stories I have switched some identities.

> Example one; Roger and Joan thought they heard the call of God to missionary work in India. They told their church, who were pleased about their enthusiasm but were wary over their lack of experience. But Roger and Joan were determined to overcome all obstacles because of their conviction that God had called them. So the church decided to support them, and raised the money to send them. For many reasons it didn't work out. Their mission failed and they were left penniless. The church had to raise further funds to bring them home. They returned to confront deep personal problems within themselves. A friend remarked in hindsight 'perhaps I or someone should have told them that their mission was foolhardy'. Perhaps someone did.

> Example two; Justin was a lay preacher and worked in a London department store. Many, both young and old, were blessed by his ministry of love and direct talking. He felt God calling him to go into full time ministry. He consulted Mary, his wife. Justin had a rock solid marriage. They consulted their church, who saw the merits of expanding his ministry but realised that he would need financial support. Accordingly a trust, independent from the church, was set up to support both his family and his ministry for life. Shortly afterwards, Justin and his wife moved to the West Country. The support moved with him. His ministry flourished. Many, including myself, have much to thank Justin and Mary for.

Following Jesus will cause us to make decisions. These might be big, earth-moving decisions, or more quiet, stay-at-home decisions. Either way we must see what this cost might involve. Luke chapter fourteen tells us that there are three costs. The first is the cost of being small. The second is the cost of being rejected, and the third is the cost of going into some uncomfortable places.

Being small

Following the theme of chapter thirteen, the first cost that Luke tells us of at the outset in chapter fourteen is the cost of being small. But being small doesn't suit everyone - in fact it's something that doesn't suit most of us. It didn't suit the prominent Pharisees with whom Jesus dined with that day (Luke 14:1). Being small was not remotely on anybody's mind and so Jesus told him:

> *When you give a luncheon or dinner, do not invite your brothers or sisters, your relatives, or your rich neighbours...so that you will be repaid. (Luke 14:12)*

I don't think for one moment that Jesus is telling the host (or us in that position) that we should stop having our friends around for supper. What he is saying is that it doesn't impress God one jot if our guest list entirely depends on building up contacts for our own prestige. Counting the cost should not be influenced by the size of someone's wallet.

Rejection

The second cost follows hard on the first. Jesus tells us about the rejection that those who follow him will suffer on account of their being small. Rejection was part of Jesus' life, and so he told one of his more famous parables to those around the Pharisee's lunch table. It begins:

> *Jesus replied: A certain man was preparing a great banquet and invited many guests. At the time of the banquet he sent his servant to tell those who had been invited, 'Come, for everything is now ready.' But they all alike began to make excuses. The first said, 'I have just bought a field, and I must go and see it. Please excuse me.' Another said, 'I have just bought five yoke of oxen, and I'm on my way to try them out. Please excuse me.' Still another said, 'I just got married, so I can't come.' The servant came back and reported this to his master. Then the owner of the house became angry. (Luke 14:16-21)*

The interpretation of this parable is not difficult to see. The man preparing the banquet was God. Those invited were the privileged sitting around the lunch table. We might debate as to whether these excuses were genuine or not but these invitees were known to the man preparing the banquet. He knew that they were busy people. He knew that one of them had just got married - yet he still invited them. So just imagine. I send out invitations to a party I am hosting to people that I know:

> JOHN BLOOR
> is pleased to invite
> BEN NEVIS
> to a banquet at his home
> on 1 March 2011.
> RSVP

I've spent hours planning, thinking about what they would like to eat, considering bar facilities, whether or not to have a disco or perhaps a live band. I've counted the cost and I am ready. A few days later the replies start coming in. They are a bit disappointing. One replies that he can't come because he has got to buy a field, Another is even more disappointing, offering a particularly lame excuse. He can't come because he has try out a couple of cows. But the one that really took the biscuit is the one I sent to Ben - who I thought was my friend but who instead replies:

> BEN NEVIS
> thanks
> JOHN BLOOR
> for his kind invitation to
> a banquet on 1 March 2011
> but would prefer to stay home with his wife.

What would you think if you got a reply like that? Well I know what I would think - that's your lot Ben. No more invitations for you. So can we be surprised that God reacts in the same way?

The anger shown by the man throwing the party was not so much that the excuses were lame but that those who refused held him in no standing. The point of this parable is that, for the invitees, there was something more important than the man giving the banquet. They considered him too small and irrelevant to their position in the hierarchy of their society. Now if we consider that the man who is giving the banquet represents God, then the full implication of the parable becomes clear. God would appear to hold no social advantages to these people, or they would have been there like a shot – wife and all!

That is why Jesus asks us to count the cost. If we are prepared to follow him, then we must be prepared to meet people who will reject us as having insufficient social standing in the same way as they rejected God – ridiculous as that might appear. But are we ready for this?

Streets and lanes

The parable continues,

> Then the owner of the house became angry and ordered his servant, 'Go out quickly into the streets and alleys of the town and bring in the poor, the crippled, the blind and the lame.' 'Sir,' the servant said, 'what you ordered has been done, but there is still room.' Then the master told his servant, 'Go out to the roads and country lanes and compel them to come in, so that my house will be full. I tell you, not one of those who were invited will get a taste of my banquet.'
> (Luke 14:21-24)

The third cost is being prepared to go out into the streets and find people in their homes. It might mean getting alongside those who are poor, and those at the end of their tether with nothing left to give and nowhere else to go – except to God. It might mean finding those who are crippled with self doubt or lack of confidence, or finding the 'sparrows' who feel worthless or the 'ravens' who feel cursed. Or it might mean finding those who are blind, who just can't see their way through their problems.

Or it might mean going out where it is utterly dark in order to find people in abject despair. I know a saint who visited a man in prison. The man had been convicted of abusing underage children – a man utterly rejected in today's society. Would you or I visit such a person? Yet this saint would visit this man every month. Sometimes the prison authorities would move the convicted man to another prison. This saint would still visit. Once they moved him to a prison at the other end of the country. God's saint still visited every month. That is going out into 'the lanes' where there is no lighting.

Have we counted the cost of following Jesus? Chapter fourteen is like a warning. It holds the same kind of feeling for me that I had as I looked out as a boy from the top floor of a double-decker bus over Jezreels Tower. If we haven't counted the cost yet then it is time to do so now before we go on any further.

CHAPTER FIFTEEN

LOST AND FOUND

...there will be more rejoicing in heaven over one sinner who repents...(Luke 15:7)

Travelling the road to Jerusalem wasn't so much a route march as a slow yet purposeful amble from town to village as Jesus stopped frequently to talk to some and heal others. Come the evening, he and all who followed came to a place where they could find something to eat and settle down. These were good times, as they sat around him as closely as possible so that they could hear the wealth of stories that he had to tell them in the light of an open fire. At the front, as near as possible, like eager children in a primary school, were the sinners – common-or-garden sinners, people who had not led lives to be proud of and who had done many wrong things. These were the ones who wanted to get closest to him, to feel the warmth of his acceptance. But then there was another group of people who stood further away, looking on in disapproval at his association with this riff-raff. Two groups of people: one group adored him while the other group despised him.

These may have been good times but they were also uncertain times as they travelled together. Those who adored him wanted a champion, whereas those who despised him wanted him gone. Each group detested the other and both groups needed a sense of reality. All needed to repent.

So he told them three stories. The first was about a sheep that got lost and the second was about a lost coin. But it was a third story that would strike home with those listening as it strikes home with us today. This was the story of two sons who in many ways represented these two groups listening to Jesus. Whether they adored him or whether they despised him, none of them would ever forget these stories and they haven't been forgotten since. He started with the story of the lost sheep.

The story of the Lost Sheep

*Suppose one of you has a hundred sheep and loses one of them.
Doesn't he leave the ninety-nine in the open country and go after the
lost sheep until he finds it? And when he finds it, he joyfully puts it on
his shoulders and goes home. Then he calls his friends and
neighbours together and says, 'Rejoice with me; I have found my lost
sheep.' (Luke 15:4-6)*

Many years ago, I was walking in Scotland. As I came down a footpath
into a valley, I saw a field of sheep, and a farmer on the road ahead of
me. Suddenly the farmer started to run into the field. He ran with
urgency. The object of his concern was one sheep on the other side of
the valley that had fallen over and couldn't get up. Quickly the farmer
was alongside. With one heave of two strong arms, the sheep was back
on its feet. The farmer began to walk back and the sheep followed him.
By the time I reached the bottom of the valley, the farmer had returned
to the path, so I asked him about the urgency of getting to the fallen
sheep. He told me that a fallen sheep that cannot right itself will fill with
gas and soon die. That is why he had had to run as fast as he could. Ever
since then I think of that farmer when I hear the familiar story of the lost
sheep.

Lost sheep are unthinking. There was this sheep, munching grass and
not looking where it was going until – oh dear - too late! Suddenly it was
on its back and helpless. Sheep seem unable to weigh up the
consequences of their actions. I think all of us have to own to times
when we can be like this. It is as if we become like children, unaware of
what is going on around us, blundering on, getting in the way or getting
lost.

However, it is also a picture of a loving God searching for us as we
bleat in our helplessness. He knows that, if he doesn't find us, we will die
- as assuredly as the sheep on the hillside would have died had the
farmer not got to him quickly. But, just as importantly, it is a story of the
pleasure it gives God when we are back safely. Jesus finishes the story
with a key message:

*There will be more rejoicing in heaven over one sinner who repents
than over ninety-nine righteous persons who do not need to repent.
(Luke 15:7)*

It might at first seem a curious ending because sheep are incapable of repentance - but the story was aimed at the group of people who got as close to him as they could as he told the story. They needed to take a reality check about themselves and repent of what they were.

The story of the Lost Coin

Jesus continued with the second story:

> *Or suppose a woman has ten silver coins and loses one. Doesn't she light a lamp, sweep the house and search carefully until she finds it? And when she finds it, she calls her friends and neighbours together and says, 'Rejoice with me; I have found my lost coin.' (Luke 15:8-9)*

The coin differs from the sheep in that it is an inanimate object. It rolled away out of sight from the person who valued it. Being inanimate, it is difficult to put blame on the coin in the way we might blame the sheep for not looking where it was going. Inanimate or not, the coin was like the fallen sheep, as it was just as incapable of returning to its owner. And it conveys the same message to us about God who is shown searching ceaselessly for that which is lost. Jesus finishes the story in much the same way as he finished the story of the lost sheep.

> *...there is rejoicing in the presence of the angels of God over one sinner who repents. (Luke 15:10)*

Once again it is a curious ending, bearing in mind that a coin is quite unable to repent. However this story was aimed at the group who stood apart in their condemnation and scorn. They too needed to take a reality check about themselves and to repent of what they had become.

The lost younger son and the lost sheep

So Jesus returned his attention to the nearest group as he began the third story of a lost young man who had wandered off like a lost sheep. It applies to anyone reading this today who feels alone and lost in this dark and puzzling world. I have highlighted those parts of this story that I want to bring out:

There was a man who had two sons. The younger one said to his father, 'Father, give me my share of the estate.' So he divided his property between them.

Not long after that, the younger son got together all he had, set off for a distant country and there squandered his wealth in wild living. After he had spent everything, there was a severe famine in that whole country, and he began to be in need. So he went and hired himself out to a citizen of that country, who sent him to his fields to feed pigs. He longed to fill his stomach with the pods that the pigs were eating, but no one gave him anything.

When he came to his senses, he said, 'How many of my father's hired servants have food to spare, and here I am starving to death! I will set out and go back to my father and say to him: Father, I have sinned against heaven and against you. I am no longer worthy to be called your son; make me like one of your hired servants.' So he got up and went to his father.

But while he was still a long way off, his father saw him and was filled with compassion for him; he ran to his son, threw his arms around him and kissed him.

The son said to him, 'Father, I have sinned against heaven and against you. I am no longer worthy to be called your son.'

But the father said to his servants, 'Quick! Bring the best robe and put it on him. Put a ring on his finger and sandals on his feet. Bring the fattened calf and kill it. Let's have a feast and celebrate. For this son of mine was dead and is alive again; he was lost and is found.' So they began to celebrate.
(Luke 15:11-24)

Give me my share of the estate

The younger son does not appear at first to be unthinking as the sheep was unthinking. He apparently took a decision to make a life for himself. Yet if we consider this more carefully, we can see that he acted just as unthinkingly as the lost sheep. He went off into the distant country without thought for the consequences. 'Younger' sons and daughters are everywhere – both young and not so young.

He set off for a distant country

This 'distant country' in our lives may not be very far away in terms of miles but it is miles away in terms of relationships. Think of a wife whose husband is rarely at home due to pressures of work and, when he is home, seems 'miles away'. Or consider the parent whose adolescent child is struggling in an obviously hopeless relationship while the child refuses to listen to any advice no matter how lovingly that advice is given. The child is like a fallen sheep, unable to get up.

Fields to feed pigs

Squandering our wealth might be squandering money but it might be frittering away our lives to addiction - perhaps to drugs, sex or gambling. It might also apply to those who borrow beyond their means, or blow away the riches of a loving relationship. There are many ways to misspend and to end up in a 'field of pigs', and it's a very smelly pigsty as the squandering is often self-inflicted.

When he came to his senses

The younger son famously 'came to his senses'. We all have to come to our senses eventually if we are to get out of whatever pigsty holds us, but this might be easier said than done. The younger son got to his feet and, in his rags, walked out of the pigsty. Fallen sheep can't do this. If we can't break the mould that entraps us then perhaps we are more like the fallen sheep after all. Realisation of our predicament is more likely to produce no more than a small, pathetic, sheep-like bleat. It is a call for help, a cry in the darkness, a plea to God to come into our helplessness because we have had enough of being stuck in the pigsty from which we can't escape.

A long way off

But the father did nothing. He let his child go and did nothing to prevent him going. As the boy squandered all he had in the distant country, his father continued to do nothing. The boy's life declined into the misery of the pigsty, and still the father did nothing. This seems unlike the story of the lost sheep where the shepherd scoured the hills for what he had lost. Yet if we consider this more carefully we will see that it is just the same. We bleat and still nothing happens. We complain of our predicament to our friends as we admit to them that we made wrong decisions - yet we still do nothing about it. But the moment we are prepared to turn to God, admit the wrong decisions and walk away from them is the moment that God is by our side even though he may still seem distant.

The fattened calf

Our sheep-like bleat to turn to God is a reality check on our lives and that we also want to get out of where we are or what we have become. This is repentance. The delight that the father has when he hears this repentant bleat is hard for us to comprehend. Yet God the father wants everything new for us. He wants us to renew our life, to be wearing the best clothes. Re-joining our Father God is like having a ring put on our finger showing that we are starting again. He wants us to have a new pair of shoes, indicating a new direction in life, and he wants us to have an abundant and enjoyable life - illustrated by feasting on the fattened calf.

The parable of the younger son is so well known because many relate to it. The pigsty represents where we are or where we might have been. It is a story of repentance. It is a story of God's delight when we are prepared to get out of our mess and wake up to the reality of God and to the reality of our life.

The elder brother and the lost coin

Jesus' story now switches away from the younger son and onto the elder brother, and in doing so he switches the attention to the group furthest away from him. This is the group who disapproved of the riff-raff around Jesus, and the story applies to anyone who scoffs and condemns in their judgment of others. The younger son has now returned and the father is throwing a party. Again I want to look at a few phrases from this part of the story:

> Meanwhile, the older son was in the field. When he came near the house, he heard music and dancing. So he called one of the servants and asked him what was going on. 'Your brother has come,' he

replied, 'and your father has killed the fattened calf because he has him back safe and sound.'

The older brother became angry and refused to go in. So his father went out and pleaded with him. But he answered his father, 'Look! All these years I've been slaving for you and never disobeyed your orders. Yet you never gave me even a young goat so I could celebrate with my friends. But when this son of yours who has squandered your property with prostitutes comes home, you kill the fattened calf for him!'

'My son,' the father said, 'you are always with me, and everything I have is yours. But we had to celebrate and be glad, because this brother of yours was dead and is alive again; he was lost and is found.'

(Luke 15:25-32)

I have been slaving for you

The elder brother is like the lost coin. Full of resentment, he thinks that his father sees him as nothing more than an inanimate object. He slaved in the field and never felt noticed. The process of his slaving had detached him from his father in the same way as the coin had become detached and rolled away. Furthermore, the elder brother saw no possible fault that could be laid at his door, any more than blame could be attached to the coin. To his mind his father was wholly to blame for causing the detachment, in the same way as the woman was wholly to blame for losing the coin.

He refused to go in

Being detached, the elder son refused the company of both his father and his younger brother. There are people in church today, and perhaps no longer in church, who have lost touch and become detached from their heavenly father, and with all outside their immediate sphere of activity. Some have become slaves to duty and have forgotten the first joy of love that they found in God. Often such people become judgmental just as the eldest brother became judgmental. In telling this story, Jesus left an open question as to whether or not the elder brother was 'found' by his father in the same way that the coin was found. Would he stay out and remain inanimate, or go in joining his younger brother in repentance and be 'found' as well?

We had to celebrate

Jesus' story shows that God is delighted to go into the party because he rejoices over the repentance of the lost son. The boy didn't want his life to continue the way it was and so he got out of the pigsty that he was in – and God whooped with delight! This means that if the elder brother also went into the party, God would be just as delighted, because the elder brother was in just as much of a pigsty as his younger brother. It is the story of God's delight when those like the elder brother wake up to their reality and walk away from their resentment, realising that they don't want to be in that pigsty any longer. There is rejoicing in the presence of the angels of God over one sinner who repents.

The words 'we had to celebrate' are crucial to deciding what happened with the elder brother. If he joined the party it would be a sign that he was prepared to forgive his brother but to stay out would indicate that he was not prepared to forgive. Which way would he go? The question remains tantalisingly unanswered, and it is left to the next chapter for us to see what the answer might have been. Jesus left the question unanswered because the same question faces each of us at various times in our life. Will we take a reality check on our lives and, in so doing, be prepared to forgive others? Or are we stuck in our own pigsty of self-righteousness, separating ourselves from God?

Our older brother

Rejoicing and celebration are common to these stories. For there to be any rejoicing, there must be an absence of judgment. There can be no rejoicing from those who blame any 'sheep' for falling. There can be no rejoicing from those who blame others for not being more careful, and there is no rejoicing from those who condemn any lost sons and daughters. This is why the invitation to the elder brother to join the party is so important. At times we all play the elder brother and, in God's eyes, we too have to come to our senses and not play the judge over the misfortune of others who, after all, are no different from ourselves.

Fortunately for us, we have an older brother and this older brother is not like the elder brother in the story. This older brother is quite prepared to get into the pigsty with us – whatever that pigsty is. This older brother is prepared to help us back to our Father. This older brother joins the party to celebrate our return. This older brother is Jesus.

Many years ago I had a dream while I was preparing to give a talk on the younger lost son. I dreamt that the younger son had returned and the celebration was in full swing. But outside were the smouldering embers of a fire. On the fire were the rags of the younger son and burning alongside were the remains of the fattened calf. It seemed to me to be a picture of the mutilated remains of Jesus on the cross, who died with my dirty rags alongside him. His death makes it possible for us to come to our senses and return home.

CHAPTER SIXTEEN

SHREWD NOT SEPARATED

And besides all this, between us and you a great chasm has been set in place, so that those who want to go from here to you cannot, nor can anyone cross over from there to us. (Luke 16:26)

Another day, another evening further down the road to Jerusalem, and Jesus dipped yet again into his abundance of stories. Yet there was something different this time - for the stories he told in chapter sixteen were to his disciples rather than to the mass of followers he addressed in chapter fifteen. It might have been that Jesus had gathered with his disciples in the open, perhaps in a market square, where others could hear what he was saying. And there were others listening, for the ears of sneering Pharisees were never far away. A huge chasm separated Jesus from the Pharisees and it was widening as each day passed.

Luke chapter sixteen contains another two stories. It opens with the parable of the shrewd manager. I can safely say that in the forty-five years that I have been a Christian, I have never heard the parable of the shrewd manager read in church, let alone preached about. It doesn't seem, at first glance, to fit with Jesus' teaching. One day, I read the parable of the shrewd manager to a Christian lady who I used to work with. I asked her 'have you ever heard this parable?' She shook her head in disbelief. 'Jesus told it,' I said, to her wide eyed astonishment. So here goes – this is a version of it adapted from Luke 16:1-7.

The shrewd manager

Mr. Rich was owner and master of an estate with some houses and flats. He employed an agent to collect the rents and manage all expenses necessary to keep the estate properly maintained and to give him an adequate return on his capital. However the master was becoming increasingly aware that the income from the estate was not what it might be and he suspected the managing agent of either not doing his job properly or worse. So on one of his site visits, the master called his manager in and told him to present the books for inspection the following day.

Now the manager knew that he was in hot water. One look at the books and his inadequacies would be revealed. He hadn't done his job properly. Unpaid debt had not been collected. In his despair he hit upon a cover-up plan. It was an outside chance. He made a few phone calls to the debtors that all went something like this:

Manager: Is that you, George?
George: Hello Bill, great time round the pub the other night.
Manager: George, I've got a problem. The boss wants to see the books. You know that £1,000 you owe in unpaid rent. Well get round here tonight, quick as you can, with £500 and I'll write the debt off.
George: Thanks Bill. But look, how's that going to work for you?
Manager: Well, I'll be OK unless he rumbles me
George: But he's bound to see through it and you'll lose your job.
Manager: Then I'll be mincemeat, George, but at least this way I'll keep my friends.
George: Bill, you've been my mate for years. I'll make sure that you'll be OK.

Now at this point I will revert to the Bible text:

The master commended the dishonest manager because he had acted shrewdly. For the people of this world are more shrewd in dealing with their own kind than are the people of the light. I tell you, use worldly wealth to gain friends for yourselves, so that when it is gone, you may be welcomed into eternal dwellings.
(Luke 16:8-9)

So what did the disciples make of this? What do we make of it? The problem with understanding this parable is in the identity of the rich man. Who does he represent? The rich man surely cannot represent God because he approved of something dishonest but, having said that, Jesus held up the quality of shrewdness in the manager as a good example. The answer is that this parable holds two deep lessons for Christians, which is why this parable is told to the disciples, with the Pharisees listening on and not to the larger crowd who were following.

Lesson one is about shrewdness – not stupidity, and lesson two is about shrewdness – not dishonesty.

Shrewdness – not stupidity

The essential nature of this wonderful gospel is that everything, absolutely everything, is connected up to what has been written before and what is written after. If we try to look at this parable of the shrewd manager in isolation, we will not be able to grasp its importance.

Chapter fifteen is about someone or something getting lost. In all cases, there was a certain amount of stupidity involved. The sheep wandered off and didn't look where it was going. The woman was careless and lost her coin. The younger son was profligate and the older brother was resentful and proud. The underlying theme of chapter fifteen is forgiveness, and rejoicing when those that were lost are found. But as ever Jesus wants to put a balance on this - forgiveness and rejoicing do not condone stupidity.

Now, if we look at the parable of the shrewd manager, we can see some parallels with the story of the lost younger son:

> They both squandered wealth
> They both found themselves in some form of pigsty
> They both turned to someone for help

In the case of the younger son, he sought help by throwing himself at the mercy of his father whereas in the case of the manager, he tried to extricate himself from his mess through a shrewd – albeit dishonest - plan involving his friends. Effectively Jesus is holding this manager up to the disciples and telling them to be shrewd. Stupidity might be forgivable but it is not acceptable if we seek to be good stewards of God's work. The disciples had to know this, and so must Christians, for being a Christian does not entitle us to be stupid.

As I write this, companies have had to make difficult decisions to keep their businesses afloat. If they don't, they will go under. This is tough but shrewd and Jesus is telling Christians that they have to be the same. This goes for anything in the Christian life - whether it concerns a project, a church service, or a meeting. Everything should be thoroughly planned and prepared. I hate it when someone says of the church 'they would never be able to do this in business'.

Christian management should always be acceptable in business. This is what Jesus is teaching us here. I despair when I hear of outreach projects that have fallen on their face for lack of hard-nosed preparation. I cringe when I witness what can be the toe-curling experience of an under-prepared church service and when I'm bored solid with church meetings that go round in circles and get nowhere. If business directors cannot be trusted to get their business right, then they will be replaced. In the same way, if Christians can't be trusted to run their church efficiently, then God will not trust them with his Holy Spirit either. This is one part of Jesus' message to us through the parable of the shrewd manager.

BUT - and the second part of Jesus message through this strange parable represents a very big 'but':

Shrewdness – not dishonesty

The rich man in the parable does not represent God. The rich man 'commended the dishonest manager because of his shrewdness', but God will not be defrauded by anybody, nor will he ever commend dishonesty. Where Jesus commended shrewdness, he also went on to say that God's law was inviolate. This is why this strange parable is followed by Jesus saying

> It is easier for heaven and earth to disappear than for the least stroke of a pen to drop out of the Law (Luke 16:17)

The parables of chapter fifteen and sixteen have a combined message. When we are in a mess, there might be two stages that we have to go through in order to get out of the mess. The first thing that we must do is to throw ourselves on the mercy of God and ask for forgiveness; and the second stage is to use all shrewdness to get ourselves honestly out of the mess we are in. The shrewd manager in the story tried to get out of his mess without going through the first stage and he couldn't achieve the second stage without being dishonest and, even then, there is a huge question mark over whether he would even manage to wriggle out of it dishonestly.

What Jesus is saying is that we have to decide to go one way or the other. We either go God's way, acting shrewdly but honestly. Alternatively we can take the dishonest route. However if we decide to take the dishonest route then we mustn't think that we can justify our mess before God as well. Jesus goes on further:

> No one can serve two masters. Either you will hate the one and love the other, or you will be devoted to the one and despise the other. You cannot serve God and Money. (Luke 16:13)

The Pharisees realised that this was pointed at them. They would have approved of the manager's shrewdness, particularly if he managed to 'get away with it'. Appearances were all important to people like the Pharisees and they would have little hesitation in bending the Law in order to justify themselves by it. Nothing much has changed for the 'Pharisees' of today.

So the Pharisees sneered at Jesus (Luke 16:14) and, in that sneer, we can see the huge gap opening ever-wider between them and Jesus. This ever-growing gap is central to the other story in Luke chapter sixteen.

The rich man and Lazarus

Jesus followed this up with a second story about separation from God. It goes something like this (adapted from Luke 16:19-31):

> Mr Rich sat back in the taxi that was whisking him to the railway station at the end of another busy day. 'Whisking' was a bit of an optimistic description that night, as the roads were full with rush hour traffic, so he had the opportunity to get out his laptop and update his impressive CV. He was one of six brothers from a middle class family and had enjoyed a good education. Over the past eight years he had worked for and been promoted within a large global corporate company. Long hours and attentiveness to detail had bought him to the attention of the national board, and now he was knocking on another promotion door toward a senior directorship and maybe even to the board itself. When that happens, he thought happily to himself, I'll start earning real money. But right then he needed his CV updated for an important

tender submission. If he could just land this one, he thought restlessly, it just might bring on that promotion.

He looked up and saw that the taxi was turning into the station forecourt. It was raining now, and he was anxious to pay off the cabbie and get inside, but as he turned he found his way barred by a beggar who operated in and around the station precinct. 'Have you got a pound for a cup of tea?' asked the beggar. Mr Rich stepped around him and, without speaking, shook his head as he walked smartly past. He had seen this beggar working the forecourt many times before. 'I've got to go into hospital next week' called the beggar to the back of Mr Rich, who lengthened his stride in order to get out of the rain. Mr Rich was irritated 'Why don't they get these people off the street?' he hissed through his teeth, but then he was comforted by the announcement coming over from the station's sound system 'Please do not give money to beggars in the station'.

The beggar was called Lazarus and he was desperate. He was cold and hungry. The hostel that he usually tried to get into was full and it looked like he was going to have to spend another night on the street. How had he got into this state? He couldn't remember. He wasn't even called Lazarus. Somebody who knew the Bible at the hostel called him Lazarus jokingly because, with all his ailments, he should have died years ago. He tried explaining to people that he had to go into hospital next week. The doctor had told him that they had to remove a lung, but no one seemed to care very much.

That was the last time that Lazarus went to the station to beg for money. He died a few days later on the operating table. The surgeon did all he could to save him but his body was simply too exhausted from years of deprivation.

Now Mr Rich was nothing. Cancer had struck unexpectedly and, within six months, he was gone. Gone from the business, his CV irrelevant, someone else senior director. He was nothing, had nothing, was loved by no one. Rich was dead – as dead as Lazarus had been six months earlier. In his nothingness, Rich saw and recognised the beggar at the railway station. He was surrounded with love and with him was someone familiar, someone he had heard of once long ago. He wanted to be there as well. He yearned for the love that the beggar was enjoying, but he found that he was barred by this huge gap or chasm that eternally separated him from them - a chasm as big as the one that had separated him from the beggar at the station. Tormented, he heard himself calling out - but the gap was too wide. Lazarus didn't hear him but the other person did. 'Tell my brothers,' Rich tried to scream, but he saw in the eyes of Abraham that his brothers had already been told, just as he had been told. Rich realised in his torment that he had not taken notice of God any more than he had taken notice of Lazarus on the station that night, or any other night. Now his desolation was complete.

Lazarus had one way out of his pigsty and that was through death. Jesus described his walk home as angels carrying him to Abraham's side (Luke 16:22). In life he was like the younger son, 'longing to fill his stomach with the pods that the pigs were eating'. In death, like the younger son, he had been lost but was found again.

But for Mr Rich it was different. He was not a bad person. He was born and was raised into a world intent on making money and living well (you've only got one life, you know). If he ever got himself into a mess, which we all do from time to time, he would have undoubtedly tried to plan his way out of it. Mr Rich would have approved of the tactics of the shrewd manager whilst at the same time hoping or possibly priding himself that he would never be taken in and defrauded by someone like that.

In many ways Mr Rich was like the elder brother in chapter fifteen. You may recall that the parable left us up in the air as to whether the elder brother went into the party or whether he stayed out. Mr Rich looked down on Lazarus in the same way as the elder brother looked down on the younger son. Regrettably the story of the rich man and Lazarus would seem to indicate that the elder brother chose to turn away from his father and away from the welcome home party. The gap or chasm between the elder brother and his father was probably too big.

Jesus was telling this story to the Pharisees who were listening and sneering, and he is telling the same story to us today. He wants to bring our attention to how much we might be like Mr Rich. In the same way, he is asking us to question how much we are like the elder brother. God wants us to realise that there is a huge gap between him and all like Mr Rich who have little time for others, particularly those they hold as being beneath their ambitions. He wants to tell us that there is a huge separation between him and all 'elder brothers' who are stiff with pride and condemnation. He wants us to realise that he is over the moon when we act shrewdly so that, when we are in a mess, we shrewdly come to a sense of reality, we shrewdly get out of whatever pigsty we have found ourselves in and shrewdly walk home to God. There is nothing, absolutely nothing, separating us from God that way.

Maybe you are asking – does this mean that, to find that narrow door to heaven, we have to speak to every beggar that approaches us? Actually it is far more serious than that. The story of the rich man and Lazarus brings us face to face with death - the greatest challenge that faces all of us. The next chapter of Luke's gospel is all about that.

CHAPTER SEVENTEEN

DEATH

The Kingdom of Heaven is in your midst. (Luke 17:21)

Death is the only event in our lives that we know is going to happen. Death happens to all, regardless of who we are. Death faced each one in the crowd following Jesus, it faced every single one of the disciples and of course it faces all of us. But Jesus, God in the world, was walking to Jerusalem to do what was impossible. At Jerusalem he would overcome death and separation from God.

Closer now to Jerusalem, and Jesus was surrounded by Pharisees. He had told an abundance of stories to the crowd of followers and then more to his disciples. Now it was the turn of the Pharisees to be around him with questions. This is a sad picture of lost people hopelessly divided from Jesus and therefore divided from God. These are the judgmental 'elder brothers' of chapter fifteen. These are the 'rich' of chapter sixteen who were doomed to oblivion. I would like to think that these Pharisees who were gathered round were not sneering as they had been. Perhaps, impressed by the authority of Jesus, they wanted to know the truth about their future, about that day when the kingdom of heaven would arrive and when the world would cease for, like everyone else, one day they would die too.

> Jesus, tell us when the kingdom of heaven is coming.
> That's the wrong question.
> What do you mean?
> It's not 'when' that should concern you. The kingdom of heaven may come anytime.
> What should concern us, then?
> You should be concerned about where the kingdom of heaven is.
> Where is it then?
> The kingdom of heaven is within you.
> (Adapted from Luke 17:20-21)

This conversation between the Pharisees and Jesus, which I have paraphrased, is very relevant to us. Many people today still want to know if there is a heaven, where they will go after they die, and many want to know if their loved ones are in a better place and will be there to greet them when they get there. So if we were to come to Jesus, as the Pharisees did, and ask him about heaven after we die, we can rightfully assume that he will give us a similar answer. We are wrong, says Jesus, to look at the kingdom of heaven as something coming in the future. The kingdom of heaven is now. It is within us.

This now opens up a question for us all to consider. What is within us? What are our priorities? What do we consider to be the most important things in our life? It is what is within that is all-important. One day the world as we know it will cease to exist, and the portents of this are there for us all to see. Before that happens it is likely that we will die. Either way, there will come a day when our world will cease to be. How will that day find us? On that day where will our priorities lie? These are the questions that Jesus asked the Pharisees sitting around him, and these are the questions that he asks us as well. Then, in order to help them and us come to an answer he said:

> On that day no one who is on the housetop, with possessions inside, should go down to get them (Luke 17:31)

In other words, imagine we are on the roof of our house at the moment that the world as we know it comes to an end. What would be our first inclination? Would it be to get downstairs and grab as many possessions as we can, or would we just get out as fast as possible? What would be our answer?

Pompeii

In AD 79, a disaster of catastrophic proportions struck an area of central Italy. A city of some 20,000 inhabitants was suddenly engulfed by a volcanic explosion which left it buried under 60 feet of ash. Pompeii ceased to exist. It was no more.

Pompeii was south of Rome, in an area on the west coast of Italy called Campania. It was the largest of the towns grouped around a mountain perched on the coast. The mountain is called Vesuvius. We tend to link the name 'Vesuvius' and 'volcano' together, but in those days Vesuvius was not considered to be any particular threat. Indeed Pompeian wall paintings subsequently excavated showed the mountain covered in trees. There was no indication of the destruction waiting within.

Pompeii, and the area around, was growing in popularity with Rome's wealthier citizens, but sixteen years before the volcanic explosion, the city was severely damaged by an earthquake. After that, many citizens decided that this was not a safe place to live and moved elsewhere - but many others decided to stay and rebuild. If they had known what was going to happen, they would have moved out as well.

The volcanic explosion was so devastating and the burial so deep that there was no question of re-inhabitation and the city became lost for about 1,500 years. In 1599, the buried city was accidentally discovered. Amateur archaeologists began digging some 150 years later but thankfully, in the nineteenth century, the professionals took over.

Guiseppi Fiorelli was a master archaeologist. Amongst his many achievements, Fiorelli realised that cavities found in the solidified ash were created by decomposed bodies. By filling the cavities with plaster, Fiorelli uncovered the last moments of the inhabitants as they were engulfed. They are not pleasant to look at.

Some bodies lie as if asleep, with their features still recognisable, but there was one that has always stuck in my mind. This body wasn't memorable because of its 'preservation' but more because of what the person was doing. He was crouching and crawling on his knees while arms and hands were clutching despairingly onto a few possessions. As I looked at this person, I realised how important these possessions were to him. In the moments when burning ash and pumice were falling all around, the citizens of Pompeii faced a stark choice - get out and live, or get the possessions and die. This person had chosen the latter and had died.

Jesus said 'on that day, no one who is on the roof of his house, with his goods inside, should go down to get them'. On the day of death, it will be what is within us that will dictate what our priorities are. Death may surprise us and those around us. It often does even when death is anticipated. As with those in Pompeii, we may have warnings of death or be oblivious to it. Either way, it will be what is within that will dictate where our heaven is.

Where is heaven?

Our heaven is within us. The Pompeian's 'heaven' was in his possessions. His 'within' dictated his actions and the consequences followed. In the same way, Jesus pointed out that, facing death, someone on a roof with possessions inside would be faced with the same decision that faced the Pompeian. Understanding this, we might now be able to make sense of what Jesus went onto say next:

> Whoever tries to keep their life will lose it, and whoever loses their life will preserve it (Luke 17:33)

The Pompeian's possessions were his 'life' - he had tried to keep this 'life' but in doing so he had died. Had the Pompeian chosen to put aside his possessions and thereby lose this 'life', then he might have lived. It follows that what is within our hearts will determine where our 'life' is.

Death faces us all in one form or another. We too must make a choice. The choice we make will depend upon what is within. It was the 'within' that determined the actions of the younger son to decide to get out of the pigsty and find his father. It was the 'within' that would determine whether the elder brother remained judgmentally aloof or whether he would join his father in celebration. It was the 'within' that divided Mr Rich from both the beggar and from heaven. These are the examples that Jesus produced and which are recorded in chapters fifteen and sixteen of Luke's gospel. So we come to chapter seventeen, where Jesus turns the gentle light of God on us once again with the questions 'what then is within each of us?'

But let us be clear what Jesus is teaching us here. Finding God's heaven is not about morals, or whether we are good people or bad people. It is about what is within each of us, and whether God is there as well.

Noah and Lot

To help us understand, Jesus referred to the story of Noah. You may recall that God decided to send a flood because he regretted that he had made man, as he saw how great their wickedness had become.

What were they up to then? The mind boggles but let it not 'boggle' for too long for Jesus tells us what they were up to. So wait for it. - those 'wicked' people spent their time

...eating, drinking, marrying and being given in marriage...
(Luke 17:27)

Well it's not exactly Cert. 18 stuff is it! Again, you may recall the story of Lot. This story may not be so familiar, but Lot and his wife and children settled in the area of Sodom and Gomorrah. These cities are renowned for their wickedness and Jesus tells us that on the date of their destruction, the wicked people of Sodom and Gomorrah were

...eating and drinking, buying and selling, planting and building.
(Luke 17:28)

WELL JESUS, WHAT'S SO WICKED ABOUT ANY OF THAT? – we may well ask.

The answer is 'nothing, absolutely nothing' - and that is the point. There was nothing there – nothing about God. These people grieved God because they were living without him. That was their 'wickedness'. Similarly, we might understand that the elder brother wasn't a particularly bad person, nor was Mr Rich. They were both going about their daily business but their lives and hearts, in one form or another, did not include God. Their 'within' was elsewhere.

'Remember Lot's wife,' (Luke 17:32) said Jesus, hammering the point home. Why should we remember Lot's wife? The story of Lot continues: God warned Lot about the ultimate destruction of Sodom and Gomorrah, so Lot decided to waste no time and get out (quite unlike the Pompeian). What was within Lot determined whether he lived or died. So we might picture Lot, his wife and his daughters, running for their lives out of the cities when suddenly Lot's wife turned and looked back. At that point, she too died.

The story is that she was turned into a pillar of salt but don't get sidetracked by the image. Instead, realise why Jesus said 'remember Lot's wife'. What she did was to display what was within her. Within Lot's wife was not God - instead, she was still 'within' Sodom and Gomorrah. Her life yearned for the life that she had just left, so she lost her life.

Finding God depends on what 'heaven' is within. You may recall that I posed the question at the end of the last chapter as to whether the story of the rich man and Lazarus means that God wants us to speak and help every beggar we come across. To think this way is missing the point. Contemptuously brushing aside beggars may be symptomatic and an example of what might be within - Jesus is telling us to bring God into our lives. He is asking us to bring God into where our heaven is. This in turn may well lead us to help more disadvantaged people because what is now 'within' makes us want to help them.

To show up people's priorities, Luke then records an incident that took place between Jesus and ten lepers in a village on the border of Galilee and Samaria. These two regions were 'at war' with each other. Jews shunned Samaritans and vice versa. At first it looks like a rather moralistic tale of gratitude and ingratitude but if we look closer we will see how it reveals what is hidden within.

Ten lepers

In a village were ten lepers, one was a Samaritan and the implication from Luke's record is that the other nine were Jews. These ten called out to Jesus for pity, and Jesus told them all to go and show themselves to a priest. They turned and as they went they found that the leprosy had gone and they were all healed. But only one of them came back to say 'thank you', and that was the Samaritan. The others didn't. So the moral of the story is that there was one nice Samaritan that we should emulate and nine ungrateful Jews that we should not emulate. We could leave the story there but I want to look a little more closely at it.

Let us go back to the beginning of the story. Jesus was passing through. He was not going to stop for long. There was a fleeting but all too brief moment when he was there, and there were ten lepers, not feuding with each other in spite of the fact that one was a Samaritan and the nine others were Jews. The reason for this is obvious: all ten faced something greater than the feud. They were all lepers.

The ten lepers made a trip into town, hoping to take advantage of that fleeting moment and to find healing. What consternation this must have caused the villagers! Eventually, after dodging several rotten tomatoes, they were saved by the arrival of Jesus. So the lepers yelled at the top of their voices, 'have pity on us!' (Luke 17:13), and Jesus had pity. It was what they wanted, and he gave them what they wanted. 'Go and show yourselves to the priests,' he called back (Luke 17:14). Effectively they needed an authorised person to declare that they were lepers no longer. You might imagine them turning away in disappointment. 'What's the point of showing ourselves to priests,' they thought, 'priests won't want to see us. We're all lepers'.

At that point something quite wonderful and something quite awful took place. The wonderful thing that happened was, as they went, they realised with astonishment that they were no longer lepers. The celebrations can only be imagined. But the awful thing then that happened was that the celebrations didn't last long. Now they were no longer lepers, they returned to being nine Jews and one Samaritan, and the old divisions re-established themselves. The very thing that kept them together was no longer there. A barrier went up where there had been no barrier before. The nine rejected the one, left him on his own, and went their own way.

So what were the nine ungrateful ex-leper Jews doing while they might have been thanking Jesus? Were they whooping it up in the local pub, or some other hot spot denied to them for so long? I might suggest that they were doing nothing of the kind. What they were doing was precisely what Jesus had told them to do - finding a priest.

And the Samaritan – what of him? He found himself alone, and it must have been a dreadful time for him, deserted by the people that he had counted on as friends. What was he to do? Like the nine he was conscious of Jesus' instructions to find a priest, but where? He couldn't go and find the same priest as the other nine because he was a Samaritan. The answer was obvious. He only knew one priest that he could show himself to and that was Jesus. When he had found Jesus, he threw himself at his feet. 'Look at me,' he must have cried with tears running down his leper-free cheeks. Jesus said 'rise and go, your faith has made you well'. (Luke 17:19)

So it is not a moralistic tale of gratitude and ingratitude at all. It's a story of a man with nowhere else to go. The Samaritan leper is like the younger son. He was now out of his pigsty and he went where he was welcome. He went to Jesus.

But the rest had other priorities.

Faith

Jesus told the Samaritan that his faith had made him well. But I think that all ten lepers must have had faith, for they all decided to find Jesus and call for pity. The difference between the nine Jews and the one Samaritan was what they each held within. Despite their faith, the nine Jews had a stronger priority that took hold once they realised that they were healed. They were now Jews first and foremost and, although there is nothing the matter with being a Jew, it caused them to raise barriers that separated them from their friend. That barrier was as great as the one between the rich man and Lazarus. The racial barrier that they raised separated them not only from the Samaritan but also from Jesus.

But there was something else about the nine, which is yet more tragic. They represent all who believe they are doing the right thing - like the elder brother. They live a decent life and make a decent living, totally missing the barriers that their priorities create. It is a most terrible delusion that at times affects all of us.

At the same time, I doubt that there was anything particularly good about the Samaritan but he had faith, enough faith to return to Jesus. It was that faith, as small as a mustard seed, which made all the difference between the Samaritan and the other nine. Who will find the kingdom of heaven? It will be those with nowhere else to go, who have a tiny bit of faith to realise it. Those who find the kingdom of heaven are those who make the kingdom of heaven a priority within themselves.

As I look into my own life I realise that there is much within that doesn't include God. I can see why so few will find the narrow door that leads to God's heaven, and I see much of the elder brother in myself. I have found that writing this chapter on death has been particularly difficult, as it has bought up all sorts of reactions and impulses within. However, there are moments when Jesus might just be passing through our lives as he passed through that little village on the warring borders of Galilee and Samaria. We need to grab those moments in our 'warring lives' and follow him. We will find others in chapter eighteen that might encourage us to understand more about faith as he walked to Jerusalem to achieve the impossible and overcome death.

CHAPTER EIGHTEEN

DEPENDENCE AND PERSISTENCE

Anyone who will not receive the kingdom of God like a little child will never enter it (Luke 18:17)

Jesus was nearer still to Jerusalem, and yet again he was surrounded, but this time not just by the crowds who followed him, or his disciples, or the Pharisees - who, as always, were not far away. This time Jesus was surrounded by young children. I'm not sure why the disciples wanted to prevent the children touching Jesus, bearing in mind that adults seemed to be literally falling over themselves to touch him, but Jesus would have none of it - saying words which, as a five year old, I first heard at school:

> *Let the little children come to me and do not hinder them, for the Kingdom of God belongs to such as these. (Luke 18:16)*

And then Jesus goes on to say something vital to us all if we want life after we die.

> *Anyone who will not receive the kingdom of God like a little child will never enter it. (Luke 18:17)*

We learned in chapter seventeen that the kingdom of God is within us, and chapter eighteen takes this a step further. The kingdom of God is within us - but for God to thrive within us we must receive him like a child. This won't be easy for some, because to accept God as a child means adopting the qualities of a child. There are two child-like qualities in particular that Jesus wants us to adopt within our character; the first is dependence, and the second is persistence.

We start with dependence and a story in chapter eighteen about two men coming to church. One was dependent on God whereas the other was not.

Dependence

They came to the church separately but arrived together. They came with one mind and with one objective. They were both intent on praying to God. It seems that they knew each other, at least one – a Pharisee – knew that the other was a tax collector, with a reputation for cheating people in order to line his own pocket. They arrived together, but as soon as they came into the church, they parted.

The Pharisee went to the front of the church and stood as he prayed. He prayed about two things. First he prayed about others, particularly praying for the other man in the church whom he had recognised as he came in. 'God, thank you that I am not like him,' he prayed. Then he prayed his second prayer, which was about himself - 'You know, God, that I am a decent man and live a respectable life. You can depend on me'. He looked at himself and saw nothing wrong.

The other man stayed at the back as far out of sight as possible. He remained in the shadows, hoping that the darkness might hide him. He wanted to pray but there was a problem. He was afraid to look at God just in case God might look at him. So with head bowed he just cried out quietly the same words over and over again. 'God have mercy on me, a sinner'. He looked at himself and saw much that was wrong.
(Adapted from Luke 18:10-13)

The humility of the taxpayer led him to a realisation that, for all his pain, any relationship he was to have with God depended entirely on God. Such a relationship is similar to the one between a young child and a parent. The young child is helpless and a successful relationship therefore depends on the parent. On the other hand, the Pharisee's dependence was based entirely on himself, and thus he deluded himself that he had some sort of relationship with God. In truth, his 'prayer' was more akin to talking to one of his mates. He didn't see God as God at all.

Jesus said: *I tell you that this man (the tax collector) rather than the other (the Pharisee) went home justified before God. For all those who exalt themselves will be humbled and those who humble themselves will be exalted (Luke 18:14)*

This story was another way for Jesus to tell the story of the lost son and the elder brother. It is probable that the taxpayer had reached a life-crisis, a pigsty by another name. He found that he had nowhere else to go other than a church and nothing else to do except cry out into the darkness, 'God have mercy upon me, a sinner'. It was in that darkness that he found the dependence that justified him before God. In spite of what he had become, he had a relationship with God and the kingdom of God was his.

The two men came to the church together with one mind and one objective. But at the church they separated and, when they left the church, they remained separated. In church the deluded Pharisee became separated from God. But the other, the tax collector, saw himself in reality and went home justified in the eyes of God.

Persistence

The kingdom of God is found in child-like dependence. It is also found in child-like persistence, and children can be horribly persistent! What parent hasn't felt the urge to wring a few necks as the little ones persist with their demands?

Luke chapter eighteen starts and finishes with stories of persistence. The chapter opens with a story of a widow who bugged the life out of some poor judge until she got what she wanted (Luke 18:1-4), and it ends with the story of a blind beggar who wouldn't stop yelling until he was led to Jesus (Luke 18:35-43).

First, the widow's persistence, which I will relate through an experience of my own:

> Nathan was an orthodox Jew, resplendent with long flowing beard and a homburg hat and he used to drive me round the bend! It wasn't that he was unpleasant, far from it - Nathan was a very friendly man. He just had a habit of ringing me for some advice and wanting to talk about the world when it wasn't convenient. I tried everything. I tried telling him that I couldn't do what he wanted me to do – that didn't work. I tried ignoring his phone calls, and that didn't work either. Nathan just persisted. The only thing I

didn't do was tell him to go away. I just couldn't bring myself to do that. So I would always find myself dropping what I thought was more important in order to give Nathan what he wanted.

Years later I was diagnosed with prostate cancer and one of the first people to call me was Nathan, who had obtained my mobile number from the office. My secretary was very reluctant about giving Nathan my number because she knew how much he drove me (and her) mad. But Nathan, being Nathan, persisted. He wouldn't let it go, and eventually my secretary relented. When Nathan contacted me he was full of concern but more than that – he was full of ideas. Nathan and my eldest son were particularly instrumental in leading me to get the best care that I could have had. I am very grateful to them both, but I look back at times and recall with much amusement how help came in my hour of need from the persistent Jewish friend who drove me mad!

The blind beggar

Closing the chapter, Luke relates another story of persistence. It is about a totally blind but very persistent beggar. Jesus was now approaching Jericho. The end of his journey was in sight, as Jericho was only about 50km from Jerusalem, probably best remembered for its walls tumbling down before an army of Israel under Joshua many, many years before. On the roadside sat a blind beggar as defenceless as the city had been without its walls – as defenceless as a child. As he sat at his place he realised that a large crowd was building up. Something was happening.. Having established that it was Jesus passing by, he took his chance. He had heard about Jesus and there was never going to be another moment like this one. So like a child, he yelled out persistently:

> Jesus, have mercy on me!
> You hear that?
> Hear what?
> That yelling!
> Oh, it's the blind beggar.
> Well, tell him to shut up. He will give us all a bad name
> Oi, you, eyesore - shut it!

Son of David, have mercy on me!
He's still yelling his head off.
Well, I can't help that.
For goodness sake tell him!
Look sunshine. Are you deaf as well? You're getting on everyone's
nerves. I said shut it.
(Adapted from Luke 18:40-41)

But the blind beggar would not shut it. In fact his persistence paid off -
Jesus heard him over the noise of the crowd and ordered that he be
brought to him.

'What do you want me to do for you?' asked Jesus (Luke 18:41), and
the blind man answered from deeply within himself.
'I want to see', he said (Luke 18:41).

This was his heaven and so Jesus gave him his heaven. But if anybody
thought that would shut him up, they were to be sadly disappointed.
Instead he followed Jesus down the road, making even more noise, as
children do, so that others saw it and joined in the din. I suspect other
eyes were opened that day to the wonder of Jesus.

Where is the kingdom of God to be found? It is to be found within each
one of us with the dependence and the persistence of a child. Firstly we
have to know that any relationship with God is dependent on God.
Secondly, God wants those dependent on him to pray persistently for
our families, for our communities, for our hometowns, for our nations
and our leaders, and for the world.

But let us not pretend that any of this is at all easy - as a rich ruler was
soon to find out.

The rich ruler

He sought to get close to Jesus, as many had done before. With his
earnest face, he persisted in asking a question that others had asked
previously. 'Good teacher, what must I do to inherit eternal life?' (Luke
18:18). According to Matthew's gospel, this man was a young man, and
he was a rich ruler. He wasn't trying to catch Jesus out - he really wanted
to hear the answer - but what followed was one of the saddest moments
in the gospel. This young earnest and devout young man was separated
from God and didn't know it.

Jesus answered the question in the same way as he had done before, going back to the Law. But as before, when challenged with this question, there was a sticking point. The young man was wealthy and that was important to him. Try to imagine the conversation between the young man and Jesus.

Jesus, I want to know what happens after I die. Is there life after death? Is there a place that we might call Heaven?
Well, that depends.
What does it depend on?
To go to God's heaven you will have to keep God's law.
I have tried to live a decent life.
OK, let's see then. Are you married?
No.
Have you had sex with anyone?
Well I've had some girlfriends, but nothing serious.
Have you ever treated anyone unfairly?
Not to my knowledge - and if anyone has had a grievance about me, I have always put it right.
Have you ever taken a sicky?
I have worked honestly and give my employer the best at all times.
Do you gossip?
I try to make certain that whatever I have to say about someone, I say it face-to-face.
When did you last see your parents?
This weekend.
How often do you see them?
I try to see them every weekend but that isn't always possible.
I understand that you are a wealthy person?
Yes, as I have said, I have worked very hard for what I have.
What if I asked you to give all your wealth to the poor?
Why should I want to do that?
In that way you will find the Heaven you seek and all its treasures.
(Adapted from Luke 18:20-22)

But that was too much. The young man went away sorrowfully. The gut-wrenching part of this is that Mark adds in his version of the story that Jesus 'looked at him and loved him' (Mark 10:21). How wretchedly sad it must have been for Jesus to watch him go. What we see in this story is a young man who was a good man. He was someone out of the top-drawer, somebody that every mother would like her daughter to marry. 'Who then can be saved?' (Luke 18:26) asked those who heard the conversation. Who then can find life after we die? If he can't – that decent young man – then who can? And Jesus replied with one of his most famous sayings, and it seemed to shut the door on all hope:

> *Indeed, it is easier for a camel to go through the eye of a needle than for the rich to enter the kingdom of God. (Luke 18:25)*

Impossible!

Impossible for man, possible for God

The rich young man had got it wrong for two reasons. The first reason was that his priorities were in his possessions. Possessions were more important to him than God. He was like the Pompeian we looked at in chapter seventeen; but there was another reason. He genuinely thought that his lifestyle made him acceptable to God. He came with the question 'what must I do to inherit eternal life?' expecting the answer to be, 'just continue as you are'. The answer he got - to sell all his possessions - revealed that he saw himself as no more dependent on God than the proud Pharisee in the temple. With that realisation he turned away from Jesus as many turn away towards other, easier priorities.

But there is hope. It was impossible for this young man to have a relationship with God, just as it is impossible for any of us to have a relationship with God. But Jesus said, as he looked at the departing young man:

> *What is impossible with men is possible with God. (Luke 18:27)*

This is central to this chapter, and central to this book. Jesus repeats the same words that the angel used when he visited Mary with the news of her pregnancy (see chapter one). We may struggle with faith. We may wrestle with the concept of dependence on God, as we seek to justify ourselves over and over again in our everyday life. We may shun the thought of persistent prayer for others and for ourselves when nothing seems to happen. Yet in our many failings, nothing is impossible with God. There is a door that Jesus leaves opens for all of us. It is a narrow door - but it is there and it is open for any or all of us to go through and find God just as we are and with all our faults.

Jesus looked at his disciples scratching their heads and wondering. So he took them aside and told them what was going to happen and how this was going to be made possible. Perhaps we might let him take us aside for a moment as well, as he tells us what he told them:

> *We are going up to Jerusalem and everything that is written by the prophets about the Son of Man will be fulfilled. He will be delivered over to the Gentiles. They will mock him, insult him and spit on him, they will flog him and kill him. On the third day he will rise again (Luke 18:31-33)*

The disciples didn't understand what he meant then, and for now maybe we don't either. So perhaps, like them, we need to follow and see just what happened in Jerusalem.

Part Four: Jerusalem

CHAPTER NINETEEN

ARRIVAL

As he approached Jerusalem and saw the city...(Luke 19:41)

They came over the hill called the Mount of Olives and looked down at
the city. At last they had arrived at Jerusalem. Ahead of them was Jesus
riding on a colt that had never been ridden before. They had brought the
animal to him after he had directed them where they would find it.
Eagerly they threw their cloaks on the colt and those who couldn't
manage to get their cloaks on its back spread them in front of the
animal's feet. And the noise...oh the noise:

*'Blessed is the king who comes in the name of the Lord' they shouted
at the tops of their voices. (Luke 19:38)*

Who were 'they' that were shouting as they came over the hill? They were his disciples who had been with him throughout his journey to Jerusalem, but they also included many who had joined them on the way. There was a man who was blind and who could now see, and he was still shouting his praise of Jesus. Nobody could shut him up. Following was a young man who had crawled recently out of his 'pigsty'. There was a woman who was still getting on everyone's nerves and a man - a tax collector - who had found forgiveness from God in a church. There was a former leper, a Samaritan, who had lost his friends but had found another, far more precious friend. There was a woman who had been healed from an embarrassing illness, and another whose bent back had been made straight. Another man whose daughter had been brought back from the dead and a woman whose dead son had been returned to her followed, and many, many more that Luke did not record ... and, of course, loads of children.

In the crowd was another man, a short man whose life had been completely changed when he met Jesus at Jericho. He too was following Jesus, singing his praise with the others, something he would have thought inconceivable a few week ago. His name was Zacchaeus.

Zacchaeus

'Zacchaeus stood up,' (Luke 19:8) relates Luke in chapter nineteen. Zacchaeus would always remember the moment that he stood up in front of Jesus, and he was remembering it now as he followed Jesus over the Mount of Olives and into Jerusalem.

The citizens of Jericho hated Zacchaeus as they hated all tax collectors. They loathed the fact that tax collectors connived with the Roman occupation and lined their own pockets from the money of those good citizens – and Zacchaeus was a chief tax collector. Being a tax collector suited Zacchaeus because the wealth it bought seemed to overcome his deformity.

Zacchaeus saw himself as deformed, just as deformed as the blind man sitting beside the road into Jericho (chapter eighteen). Only it wasn't blindness that deformed Zacchaeus - he could see perfectly well. Lack of height was his deformity, and Zacchaeus hated being short. People laughed at him, or so he thought. If Jesus just happened to come to him and asked him what he most wanted, as he had done to others,

Zacchaeus would have answered 'I want to be tall'. Then he wouldn't have to look up at anybody any more.

The day that Jesus arrived in Jericho took Zacchaeus by surprise. He had heard about Jesus and now suddenly he was gripped with the desire to see what Jesus looked like. Appearances were very important to Zacchaeus. But he wasn't the only one who wanted to see Jesus that day. As ever, Jesus was surrounded by crowds of people and that took the little man by surprise. Not for the first time, he found that he wasn't tall enough to see. So he did something that he hadn't done since he was a boy. Driven by the moment and without any thought of the consequences, he climbed a tree – a sycamore-fig tree.

As Jesus passed by, Zacchaeus didn't shout out as the blind man had shouted out. He stayed quiet, hoping no one would see him up a tree like a naughty child. But Jesus looked up, and saw him there, and just said 'Zacchaeus, come down immediately' (Luke 19:5). Feeling utterly foolish, Zacchaeus came down - but Jesus didn't leave him there in his discomfort. Instead, he said 'I must stay at your house today,' (Luke 19:5) and the short man, overcome with surprise and delight, took Jesus into his home.

That evening Zacchaeus 'came down' in more than one way. With Jesus in his house he came down from everything that propped up his insecurity and his lack of self-esteem. He came down from his pride, he came down from his ambition, in fact he came down from every pedestal that he had built for himself over the years.

And then he stood up.

For the first time in many, many years Zacchaeus stood on his own feet. No longer was he supported by his wealth, or by his status or even by a sycamore-fig tree. Zacchaeus stood and Jesus, seated as he was at the dinner table, looked up at him. The moment that Zacchaeus stood up he realised what he had needed most in his life. He was his own man and, at last, free of everything that had driven his life before. Zacchaeus at last had found who he truly was.

But outside Zacchaeus' house it was dark. Not only had the sun gone down but there was darkness in people's hearts. These people could not bring themselves to understand that Jesus had come to save those who were lost. He had come into Zacchaeus' home and his pigsty but out there, in the darkness, people were muttering their own brand of disapproval. These were the 'elder brothers', judging the triumphant

Zacchaeus outside his home. They were also there as Jesus came down in triumph from the Mount of Olives and into Jerusalem.

Coming down the Mount of Olives

Peace in heaven and glory in the highest! (Luke 19:38)

They praised him for his miracles and continued to lay their cloaks in front of the colt that was carrying Jesus into Jerusalem.

There was another time long ago in fields outside:

Bethlehem on the night that he was born, when crowds of angels had sung something similar to what the crowds cried now: 'Glory to God in the highest heaven, and on earth peace to those on whom his favour rests!' (Luke 2:14). This time, the 'angels' that were singing Jesus' praise were men, women and children coming down with him from the Mount of Olives and into Jerusalem. As they descended, the people of Jerusalem looked up and heard the noise and, seeing the dust rising into the sky, they knew that something was happening.

The Pharisees, never far away, were voicing their disapproval of the noise. 'Tell them to be quiet!' they shouted at him through the din, holding their ears, but Jesus had no intention of telling them to be quiet. 'If they keep quiet, the stones will shout out,' (Luke 19:40) he called back, but they probably never heard him – they rarely did.

Then he stopped and looked down on Jerusalem and, seeing the darkness of the world all around him, he broke down and wept. This was hardly what his followers expected from their leader in his moment of triumph but then Jesus rarely did what they expected. This city, where he was about to be crucified, was soon to be destroyed but they didn't know or even remotely understand. He was coming into a city that thought itself chosen by God, but soon it would not have one stone left upon another, such would be the devastation of its destruction.

History records that about 40 years later, Titus, son of the emperor Vespasian, would do what Jesus had predicted. Jerusalem fell after a long and terrible siege. In Rome there is an arch in the forum (Foro Romano) called the Arch of Titus. It was built to commemorate the fall of Jerusalem and the victory of Rome over its enemies.

The story of the ten minas

As Jesus looked down and wept his mind may have returned to his time in the house of Zacchaeus. Perhaps he recollected that it had been a wonderful party, full of happiness and laughter intermingled with questions. Those around the dinner table knew that Jesus would soon enter Jerusalem. There was much about that city which was dark, worldly and ruthless. Surely, they thought, when Jesus entered that city the kingdom of God would come. So, yet again, Jesus told them a story. It is still a very up-to-date, almost twenty-first century tale. How might Jesus have told the same story if he told it today?

Tom was to be promoted to UK Managing Director of his French-owned company. He had been summoned to Paris, and he would be away for some time whilst he underwent a period of training as well as meeting other leading directors within the worldwide group. Tom was not a popular man with some of his co-directors due to his tyrannical ways, but it was his ruthless drive for profit that had attracted him to the board in Paris. Before he departed, he brought his co-directors together. They were already aware of his forthcoming promotion and were a bit wary of what this meeting was about, but they were met with the smile of a worldly, successful man.

'Look,' said Tom 'I've been in discussion with the Financial Director and had it confirmed from Paris that we can re-allocate some resources. So I am giving you each an extra budget allowance of £100,000. Use it to increase our client base'. And with that, he departed. When he had gone, some, but not all, of the directors breathed a great sigh of relief at his absence. The malcontents amongst them conspired together in order to plot a smear campaign rubbishing Tom's reputation, in an attempt to prevent his appointment as UK Managing Director.

However, the appointment was confirmed. When Tom returned from Paris, he called his directors in one by one. The first in was the Director of UK Marketing. 'What have you done with the extra investment of £100,000 I gave you before I went to Paris?' demanded Tom. The marketing director looked at Tom and realised that his job was on the line. 'You remember those five clients that we have been trying to get for some years now? Well, we induced them to attend a marketing seminar through a no-expenses-spared entertainment evening – a real boy's night out in a club and five star hotel. They've all been teetering on the brink of giving us their account and I can tell you that, so far, we have managed to sign three of them up. Those three alone are worth about a million pounds in fees just for this year.'

Tom was on his feet in a second with his hand stretched out. 'That's fantastic!' he said. 'Look, I need you to take over the City Agency and Middle-East departments as well.' Glowing within himself, the first director left Tom's office.

The second director then came in and Tom went through the same examination. 'We weren't sure,' said the second director, 'but we felt that taxi advertising might pay off. And it did. We brought in two new clients with fees worth around half a million.'

Tom remained seated. 'Well done,' he said 'Look, you've done OK. I need someone to overlook Human Resources as well. Are you up to it?' The second director left, leaving the door open for the third director - in charge of Quality Control - to walk in and slump in the chair opposite Tom. No questions were needed. 'Look,' said the third director before Tom could open his mouth, 'your £100,000 stinks as much as you stink. It is still in my budget where you left it.'

Tom said nothing. He merely reached for the buzzer under his desk top. Within moments the firm's security guards were in the room and the third director was promptly escorted off the premises, never to return.

Tom did two further things before he went home that night. Firstly he asked the first director back in and told him to take over Quality Control in addition to his other duties. Then he sacked the directors controlling City Agency, the Middle-East and HR, all of whom had conspired to plot his downfall. (Adapted from Luke 19:12-27)

The story of the minas is a story of Jerusalem in the first century AD. It is also a story of business in most major cities in the twenty-first century AD. It is a story about the world that we live in. It is as if Jesus were approaching London today, instead of cosmopolitan Jerusalem 2000 years ago. He is telling us through this story that we live in this world and at times it is not a nice place to live. We are to work in it to the best of our ability but it won't last forever - any more than Jerusalem would last forever.

Jesus wept over Jerusalem because of the world its people inhabited, a ruthless world lacking both love and the presence of God. He wept because no one in that city had any idea that they were soon to be destroyed. It is no different now. The world that we live in will come to an end, just as Jerusalem would come to an end, just as Pompeii ceased to be. Nothing will go on forever except God. Jesus wept because the people of Jerusalem were unaware of this as they went about their daily business.

The parable of the minas is not a story about God's acceptance or condemnation of anyone's work practice. Far from condemning, he is looking to find any who, like Zacchaeus, are up some sort of tree, going nowhere. Whatever our circumstances, Jesus wants to say to us, 'come down. I must stay with you today.'

He did not condemn Zacchaeus, nor did he wish to condemn anyone else. Rather, he wants us to be able to stand on our own feet and find what is permanent, instead of staying rooted in a system that will not remain.

Jesus in the temple

Jesus had arrived in Jerusalem and he went to the temple area. He had a job to do. This Temple of Jerusalem was a sacred place, constructed on a narrow promontory where God had ordained that he would meet his people through a holy priesthood. When Jesus wept over Jerusalem, he wept because he saw the misery of the world without God; but the Temple was a true shock to him. Jesus raged within himself over what he saw. The Temple was a market place. The Temple had become just another part of the world without God.

Was it not possible for men to leave just one little promontory on the world's surface as sacred to God? Couldn't there just be a few tiny acres that God could still proclaim as good? Does the world of Tom, a world of profit and ruthlessness, have to pervade everywhere? Isn't there somewhere that can be set apart?

The answer is yes – there is a place that can be set apart for God - but it was not in this Temple. The Temple of Jerusalem had had its day and it was well past its sell-by date. The Temple was to be destroyed along with Jerusalem forty years later. The Temple of Jerusalem, where God and man came together, had to be replaced with another Temple, and Jesus' aim was to make it possible for God to dwell in a sacred place where the world could not touch it. That sacred place is where the kingdom of heaven is – within us. The new Temple would no longer be a building, but would be in the hearts of those who have accepted God. The new Temple would be within those who accept all that Jesus was about to do and achieve over the next few days.

In the meantime he cleared the existing Temple out. He drove the market away, back into the world where it belonged. When they had gone, just for a moment, the Temple on the hill in Jerusalem returned to being a place sacred to God, as it was meant to be, but it would be only for a moment. Then the traders would return.

CHAPTER TWENTY

CRUSHED

...anyone on whom (the cornerstone) falls will be crushed (Luke 20:18)

Opposition can often be painful. Many would say that opposition is necessary in order to sharpen us up. In the main, I tend to agree with this sentiment; but opposition from those who set out to destroy is quite another matter. Sometimes we think mistakenly that we can withstand this type of destructive opposition, and may openly boast about how we will deal with it - but, when it comes, we find ourselves weak, helpless and without support. In fact destructive opposition can often crush the very spirit within us. Being crushed in spirit can have catastrophic effects. As a result, we lose our freedom as we find ourselves

Crushed by lack of confidence
Crushed by guilt
Crushed by self indulgence
Crushed by stress

Jesus warns us at the end of chapter twenty to be careful of those who don't mind who they crush on the way to getting what they want. Not only did he tell us to watch out for them, he also told us what they were like. They come in all types but, one way or the other, they hold these characteristics:

They are obsessed with the way they dress
They always want to be at the centre of attention
They would happily rob a widow if it were to their advantage
They believe that appearances are paramount
(Adapted from Luke 20:46-47)

Jesus met crushing opposition in chapter twenty, and overcame it in a way that we would love to be able to. Those who opposed Jesus wanted to crush him as they had crushed others, but they finished up being crushed themselves. Jesus compared himself to a stone, a huge stone, a cornerstone, which provided the top or ceiling of a monument. He said,

The stone the builders rejected has become the cornerstone. Everyone who falls on that stone will be broken to pieces, but anyone on whom it falls will be crushed (Luke 20:17)

The bullies who rejected Jesus found that this wasn't an idle threat as they confronted him after his arrival in the Temple.

Jesus in the Temple

Jesus had come to his Temple, and throughout the next few days he stayed there. He had cleared out the market place inside, and it is difficult to imagine any trader trying to get back inside while he was still there. There were a few days before the Feast of Unleavened Bread in preparation for the Passover – just a short time before he would achieve what he came to do. Until then, he remained throughout each day in the Temple. It must have caused uproar. The Temple system was in tatters. People were flocking into the city for the Passover to make sacrifices, probably ill-prepared to pay the extortionate prices for sacrificial animals that would be charged in the Temple marketplace. But this year was different. They wouldn't find the market-stalls in the Temple like they had done before. Possibly they might have found some stalls set up hastily outside the Temple precincts, but none inside - and all because of one man. But then that man was God in this world.

So imagine him for one moment, sitting in the Temple as he had done as a boy of twelve years old, teaching all who would listen to him (chapter two). Now he would teach them what was going to happen (chapter twenty-one), but each day, as he taught, he would be interrupted by questions from the opposition – destructive questions from those who wanted to crush him. These questions came from the chief priests and the teachers of the law, as they tried to catch him out. Just imagine how they planned his destruction.

Question one: authority
Chief priest:	We've got to do something.
Lawyer:	Yes, but what?
Chief priest:	I've invested a lot of money in that temple.

Lawyer:	Yes. I mean just who the hell does he think he is?
Chief priest:	He acts like he's God Almighty!
Lawyer:	That's it!
Chief priest:	What's it?
Lawyer:	That's where we'll get him.
Chief priest:	What are you talking about?
Lawyer:	He thinks that he's God Almighty.
Chief priest:	Yes – so?
Lawyer:	Well, we'll challenge him on his authority.
Chief priest:	'By what right are you here in this Temple?'
Lawyer:	*Our* Temple?
Chief priest:	But we must all go.
Lawyer:	Chief priests
Chief priest:	Lawyers
Lawyer:	Leaders of the people
Chief priest:	A show of strength.
Lawyer:	We'll put an end to his little game
Chief priest:	Just see if we don't.

Luke's account reads:

One day as Jesus was teaching the people in the temple courts and proclaiming the good news, the chief priests and the teachers of the law, together with the elders, came up to him. 'Tell us by what authority you are doing these things,' they said. 'Who gave you this authority?' He replied, 'I will also ask you a question. Tell me, John's baptism - was it from heaven, or of human origin?' They discussed it among themselves and said, 'If we say, 'From heaven,' he will ask, 'Why didn't you believe him?' But if we say, 'Of human origin,' all the people will stone us, because they are persuaded that John was a prophet.' So they answered, 'We don't know where it was from.' Jesus said, 'Neither will I tell you by what authority I am doing these things.' (Luke 20:1-8)

At first glance it seems that Jesus sidestepped having to reply. Should he not have answered the question put to him before he posed one of his own? Why did the chief priests and the lawyers not insist that he do so? The answer is that, in his response, Jesus merely went back to his credentials, which we looked at in chapter three.

John the Baptist pointed the way forward to Jesus. His authority came from John and from God. If the chief priests and the lawyers accepted John the Baptist and all that he stood for, then they would have to accept Jesus' authority. If they didn't accept John (which they didn't) then they were in trouble with the crowd around them. As far as Jesus was concerned, there was little point in answering any question concerning his authority from those who adamantly refused to accept it. So the chief priests and lawyers had to back off and keep quiet.

Silenced! Back to the drawing board.

Question two: tax

Lawyer:	Well, that didn't work.
Chief priest:	Whose fault was that?
Lawyer:	We just looked like idiots!
Chief priest:	We've got to think of something else.
Lawyer:	I thought of the last idea so it's your turn now.
Chief priest:	Well, I do have an inkling of a plan...
Lawyer:	Come on – what is it?
Chief priest:	Tax.
Lawyer:	Tax?
Chief priest:	Yes. Tax.
Lawyer:	Listen, we're talking about getting that man out of the Temple, not screwing the populace for more tax. We've got that on the agenda for next week.
Chief priest:	No, listen! We all agree that tax is always the most unpopular subject in anybody's mind – yes?
Lawyer:	Go on...
Chief priest:	That tax is the one thing that gets them all worked up...
Lawyer:	I think I'm following you. We trap him into saying that tax is OK?
Chief priest:	You got it!
Lawyer:	Genius! That way the crowd will do the job of getting rid of him for us!
Chief priest:	But we can't appear to be involved. If he sees us, he'll smell a rat.
Lawyer:	We've got to send someone he doesn't know.

Chief priest: There's some resting actors working for me. They can act as our spies.

Luke's account reads:

> *'Teacher' asked the spies to Jesus 'we know you speak and teach what is right, and that you do not show partiality but teach the way of God in accordance with the truth. Is it right for us to pay taxes to Caesar or not?' He saw through their duplicity and said to them 'Show me a denarius [roman currency]. Whose portrait and inscription are on it?' They replied 'Caesar's.' Jesus said to them, 'then give to Caesar what is Caesar's and to God what is God's'. They were unable to trap him in what he had said in public. And astonished by his answer, they became silent. (Luke 20:21-26)*

Silenced! Back to the drawing board.

Question three: the impossible question

Still plotting, the chief priests and lawyers were now joined by the Sadducees (an ancient sect who denied the resurrection):

Sadducee:	What did you think you were playing at?
Chief priest:	You try and do any better!
Sadducee:	You're all barking up the wrong tree.
Lawyer:	What do you mean?
Sadducee:	Look, you spend all your energies on trying to trip him up. That will never work.
Chief priest:	Well, what will work?
Sadducee:	All you have to do is ask an impossible question about life after death.
Lawyer:	But you don't believe in life after death!
Sadducee:	No, it's a ridiculous notion, but he teaches there *is* life after death.
Chief priest:	So, what you are saying is that we ask him an impossible question...
Lawyer:	...about life after death.
Chief priest:	...and when he can't answer it
Sadducee:	...he'll look stupid. Exactly!

| **Lawyer:** | Genius! What's the question? |
| **Sadducee:** | Oh it's a cracker. You'll see. |

Luke's account reads,

> *'Teacher' (asked the Sadducees to Jesus) 'Moses wrote for us that if a man's brother dies and leaves a wife but no children, the man must marry the widow and raise up offspring for his brother. Now there were seven brothers. The first one married a woman and died childless. The second and then the third married her and in the same way the seven died, leaving no children. Finally the woman died too. Now then, at the resurrection whose wife shall she be, since the seven were married to her?' (Luke 20:28-31)*

It is most certainly a cracker, isn't it! This is the classic 'what if' question. It's the sort of question that many today, wanting to feel superior, might love to ask without seeking or expecting an answer. It's the sort of question that must have sent Jesus' eyes rolling skyward – but he answered the question. As the question is complex, so the answer is not easy to grasp:

> *Jesus replied, 'the people of this age marry and are given in marriage. But those who are considered worthy of taking part in the age to come and in the resurrection from the dead will neither marry nor be given in marriage, and they can no longer die, for they are like angels. They are God's children, since they are children of the resurrection. But in the account of the burning bush [in Exodus chapter three], even Moses showed that the dead rise, for he calls the Lord, the God of Abraham, and the God of Isaac, and the God of Jacob. He is not a God of the dead but of the living for to him all are alive' (Luke 20:34-38)*

To any balanced, thinking person, this question verges on the idiotic but, nevertheless, it inspired an intriguing answer from Jesus about heaven. The essence of Jesus' answer is straightforward – heaven is not the same as the world we live in. Marriage, whether in wedlock or living in partnership, is an essential social structure of this world - but there is no similar marriage structure in heaven. The structure of heaven is different.

Heaven is a place structured for the living. It is for those who are resurrected into a new life just as Jesus was to be resurrected into a new life. In that new life we will be joined, through Jesus, to all who have also been resurrected to this new life. In heaven's structure, we will be joined to those great ones who first found God's hand reaching out to them. We will be joined with Moses, and with Abraham, Isaac and Jacob. We will be joined, through Jesus, to our wives, husbands and loved ones who are also resurrected and alive through Jesus. This 'impossible' question posed by the Sadducees brought forth a wonderful answer but the question, in itself, was quite irrelevant.

As I read the account of these questions and the responses received, I couldn't help thinking of Tom and Jerry cartoons. Tom was always thinking of ways to catch Jerry but he never actually succeeded. The chief priests, lawyers and the Sadducees looked as ridiculous as Tom. They knew that they had lost the battle of words. They realised that they could try as many times as they liked - they would not be able to catch Jesus out. They were simply no match for him. Three times they were silenced, crushed by his answers. Luke records that, after the third 'crushing', some of them even praised Jesus - did they mean it or were they being sarcastic? It is difficult to say, but we do know from what Luke writes in the Acts of the Apostles (the sequel to his gospel) that some Pharisees, for all their opposition, did in fact become Christians. But these, who would crush Jesus with destructive questions, would have to try something else - something less subtle. They had to get him off the street, get him out of the Temple. They had to find some way to kill him.

The tenants of the vineyard

What were they trying to defend, these chief priests, lawyers and Sadducees? What were they trying to protect? In the middle of their questioning, Luke recounts a well-known parable of the tenants of a vineyard, which sheds light on the way they were thinking.

The story that Jesus told was of a man who planted a vineyard and let it out to some tenants. When the fruit was due for harvesting, he sent a servant to collect some of the produce – a return on his investment, you might say. But the servant didn't receive a happy welcome. Instead of giving him some fruit, the tenants decided to beat him up and send him back. Other servants got the same treatment. The owner of the vineyard realised that the only way to resolve the situation was to send his son to the vineyard. Perhaps he might get a more cordial welcome. But when the tenants saw the son approaching, they saw their chance. If they killed the son, they reasoned, the vineyard would be theirs. So that is what they did. They killed him (adapted from Luke 20:9-15).

Through the many times that I have heard this story read in church, I have always had a sneaking sympathy for the tenants. Of course what they did to the servants and the son was terrible, but who can blame them for not wanting to pay the rent? Who can blame anyone? They worked hard in that vineyard - why should some absentee landlord have any of its produce? But the truth behind this story is very different. As he told the story, I think Jesus was thinking of a passage from Isaiah chapter five:

> I will sing for the one I love
> a song about his vineyard:
> My loved one had a vineyard
> on a fertile hillside.
>
> He dug it up and cleared it of stones
> and planted it with the choicest vines.
> He built a watchtower in it
> and cut out a winepress as well.
> Then he looked for a crop of good grapes
> but it yielded only bad fruit (Isaiah 5:1-2)

The vineyard in Isaiah chapter five, reflected in Jesus' story, was not a well-maintained working enterprise. It was a broken-down wreck; and its fruit, if there was any, was wild and useless. It is a picture of the Temple of Jerusalem, which was built to honour God, but was dishonoured by those who managed it. The tenants in the story did not kill to defend a productive vineyard for themselves, but rather they killed to prevent the owner finding out the truth; and the truth was that they had allowed God's 'vineyard', so lovingly planted, to fall into ruin. The story was aimed at the chief priests and lawyers who were trying to protect a way of life that had become a sham.

Foolishness

The story of the tenants in the vineyard is a tragic story of human foolishness, as they tried to defend the indefensible. It refers to the foolishness of the chief priests and lawyers who saw Jesus as a threat to their management of the Temple. But it is also about our foolishness whenever we try to kill all contact with Jesus in order to keep him out of the structure of our lives - particularly if the structure has broken down.

However this is also about the foolishness of God! We must ask from this story just how many servants had to be beaten up before the landlord recognised that the behaviour of his tenants was intolerable. Yet far from seeming convinced, he sent his son, with inevitable consequences. The foolishness of God is that, in spite of the way we are, he sent his son Jesus to us. Instead of turning his back on us he lives in the hope that, one day, we will face up to the reality of our 'vineyard'.

The stone

The opposition had forced itself rudely into the presence of Jesus as he taught in the Temple. The bully boys had come; but they met more than their match. They were crushed – painfully crushed. But Matthew's gospel adds something else:

> The stone the builders rejected has become the cornerstone. The Lord has done this and it is marvellous in our eyes.
> (Matthew 21:42)

What could be marvellous about being crushed by a cornerstone? The very thought of a huge stone falling on us is the stuff of nightmares. Certainly the 'crushing' that the chief priests and the lawyers received was no marvellous experience for them. One by one they were humiliated by Jesus; but worse than that, they were humiliated in the presence of the crowd.

Conversely, it must have been wonderful for the crowd looking on to see and hear Jesus deal with their oppressors. So in the same way, it is marvellous to have Jesus within and beside us, freeing us from the things in our lives that crush us. It is marvellous to be released from lack of self-confidence, released from guilt and from the effects of stress. Jesus teaches us in chapter twenty of Luke's gospel not to be like the self-indulgent tenants trying to defend their wrecked vineyard. Jesus comes to us in order to free us from whatever crushes us but, for him to do this, we must face the reality of what is within and not keep him out.

CHAPTER TWENTY ONE

PAUSE

...my words will never pass away (Luke 21:33)

'As Jesus looked up, he saw...' (Luke 21:1) These are the opening words of Luke's gospel, chapter twenty-one. What did he see? He saw people putting money into the Temple treasury, the rich leaving their gifts and a poor widow giving out of her poverty. He also saw those gathered around him who had been waiting for him in the Temple since early that morning. He looked up and saw these and for a moment he paused.

Luke chapter twenty-one is a pause in the action. Jesus had travelled to Jerusalem and was on the verge of achieving the impossible. He was about to make it possible for us to have a relationship with God, for us to know him as Father just in the same way as he knew God as his Father. He was going to make this possible for those he saw as he looked up – those representing both rich and poor alike, no matter what their colour or religion.

But as he paused, he saw something else. He saw that everything was passing away and nothing seen would remain; neither the people putting money in the treasury, nor the people who surrounded him, nor even the Temple, nor Jerusalem, nor the world beyond Jerusalem – it would all go. All that would remain would be God, for God is eternal and Jesus was bringing God to us so that, with God, we might be eternal as well. Tomorrow he would make this possible but for now he paused, looked up and saw.

The end of the age

Beyond the people, beyond the Temple, beyond Jerusalem to the world of God's creation – he saw to the end of the age, the end of all we know. He looked up and saw the disciples gazing in wonder at the Temple building. This caused him to repeat his prophecy that, beautiful as the Temple might be, it was soon to be destroyed. But the destruction of Jerusalem was merely a foretaste of the destruction of the world.

Alarmed, the disciples asked the question that we might have asked. 'When will these things happen?' (Luke 21:7). In answer, Jesus gave them some signs to look for, telling them that just as summer follows winter, the age of man will one day come to an end:

> Earthquakes, famines and pestilences in various places and fearful events. (Luke 21:11)
> Those that will lay hands on you and persecute you. (Luke 21:12)
> You will be betrayed, even by parents, brothers, relatives and friends. (Luke 21:16)
> Jerusalem will be surrounded by armies and you will know that desolation is near. (Luke 21:20)
> Nations will be in anguish and perplexity at the roaring and tossing of the sea. (Luke 2125)

All these things will happen, said Jesus, and he looked up and saw fear in their eyes.

Recently I bought a newspaper with a front page referring to research by the Mental Health Foundation, which involved over 2,000 people and concluded that the United Kingdom is a nation living in fear. The main reasons for our fear, according to the research, were terrorism, MRSA and flu. The research also concluded that attempts by government to allay our fears only seemed to make matters worse.

We can dismiss this research, if we want to, as yet another study like the hundreds which litter our papers each day of the week. Each day we are told that research shows that we are the best nation in the world for doing what we shouldn't and the worst nation in the world for doing what we should. We are among the fattest, we are the worst parents, we are the playground of drunkards, and so it goes on.

The research indicated that there are seven million people in the country suffering from anxiety disorders, which is 800,000 more than in 1993. What does this say to us? Does it surprise us or does it tell us what we already know? For me, one way or the other, it shows that things are no different today than they were when Jesus looked up and saw the faces of his disciples gathered around him in the Temple. So let us look at the signs that Jesus told us about and see their relevance to our lives today.

Signs

I find that writing or speaking about the end of the world presents a problem. The sun has risen over this world at least 720,000 times since Jesus said these words, so we tend to assume that it is likely to rise over the world a few more times yet. What is more, talking about the end of the world conjures up, at least in my mind, some unwashed old man with a huge beard and a bald head walking up and down Oxford Street with a sandwich board yelling 'repent – the end is nigh'. Some have predicted the end of the world, and have looked rather foolish when it hasn't happened at the time they predicted. So I suggest that we come away from thinking about the end of the world, and consider what these signs might mean to us living in a world that seems, for the present, to be alive and kicking.

Earthquakes

I have never experienced an earthquake, at least not one of which I was aware. Many years ago there was a tremor when I was on holiday in Crete. Although the earth moved, I slept through it! But I think the predominant fear about earthquakes is stability. The expression 'having one's feet on the ground' is commonly used - but what if the very ground that we are standing on is shaking? Anxiety is created by our various perceptions of safety. Do we feel safe in our houses or worried about intrusion? Do we feel that our streets are safe, or are we worried about terrorist attacks? How many of us have witnessed gangs of young people or children running around the neighbourhood seemingly out of control? How many of us have witnessed crime and beatings but were afraid to get involved? For many diverse reasons there are times when the very ground we stand on seems to shake.

Persecution

Persecution is a term that we tend to associate with religious opposition but it is far more widespread. Modern day persecution is against non-conformity, against race, against sexual inclinations, and against those who don't seem to quite fit into the neighbourhood the workplace or to our culture.

Betrayal

Jesus was about to be betrayed, as we shall see in the next chapter, and betrayal is a commonplace experience to many. Betrayal is rife in the workplace, as redundancies resound across every strata of the workforce. A man or woman comes to work in much the same way as they have been coming to work for years, only to be told without warning that they are no longer wanted and that they are to pack up their possessions from their desk and to leave the premises immediately. For many it's like being thrown out of home. Betrayal is felt by those who have worked faithfully over decades for a firm only to have their loyalty rewarded with minimum severance payments. It may be legal but it's also betrayal!

Surrounded

Jesus talked about Jerusalem being surrounded by armies (and very soon that would happen), but many today feel surrounded, not by armies but something else that makes us feel equally helpless. To some the 'army' that surrounds them is debt. In good times it might have felt safe to repay debt incurred in mortgages or purchase agreements, but when financial hardship looms through incapacity or economic breakdown, many feel encircled by an implacable enemy. To others the 'army' that surrounds them is addiction, and to others there is a more literal encirclement of inconsiderate neighbours. Feeling surrounded can come in many forms but, whatever form it takes, encirclement leaves us feeling that there is no escape. We are surrounded.

The roaring and tossing of the sea

Somebody close to me told me of a recurring dream of being swamped by waves in the sea. The drowning sensation is a horrible one that might be caused by stress through overwork, through pressure of deadlines. Life seems like being chased by an oncoming wave looming ever larger with more and more insatiable demands.

My words will never pass away

These are all familiar signs in the world today; yet all these things are passing away. Which brings us to the question that millions have asked before: 'if all these signs are there to demonstrate that all that I am, all that I think and all that I do is passing away; if this demonstrates that all around me, my family, my community, my country, and my world are also passing away, then what is the point of it all? What is the point of anything?'

But Jesus looked up and saw. He saw our great need for freedom, which cannot be contained in the wink of life but must be free to continue into eternity. So Jesus gave one of his greatest promises:

> *Heaven and earth will pass away, but my words will never pass away (Luke 21:33)*

What he is saying firstly is that everything will go at some time or other. This might be painful but it is realistic. It is the second part of the promise that gives us what we most desire. Jesus tells us that God will never pass away. Jesus is God in the world and all that Jesus has said about God will never pass away. What Jesus would do on the following day in Jerusalem will also never pass away.

The widow and her copper coins

Jesus looked up and saw. He saw a widow put two copper coins into the Temple treasury – all that she had to live on. Jesus said of her that in comparison to the rich who left their gifts, 'I tell you the truth, this poor widow has put more in than any of the others' (Luke 21:3). It's a cosy little story, seemingly about a nice generous lady, perhaps somebody that we would like to know – but what has it to do with the end of the age?

It might be a cosy story but it is also a puzzling one. We might ask, what is the point of what she is doing? Why is this poor widow putting all her money into the temple treasury? It might be very laudable but what did she do then? Did it mean that she had to sponge off her neighbours? By praising the actions of this generous woman, is Jesus advocating that we should be equally generous and give all our money away so as to live off state benefits?

We have to look beyond the obvious - beyond the money. The quality that this widow was showing as she put in her literal two-penny-worth was her dedication and her loyalty. She was putting all her money into coffers to support the upkeep of a building that was soon to be destroyed.

This woman represents mothers dedicated to the children who will one day leave them. This widow represents all teachers dedicated to inspiring young minds before they leave to take their place in the world. This woman represents all who are dedicated to the place of work that one day might make them redundant; she represents all those dedicated to their football clubs even when they lose. This widow represents those most dedicated to their military unit when they have suffered losses. She represents those dedicated to their churches even when the church seems to turn its back on them.

Yet all these things will pass away

Only God will not pass away, so there is only one dedication we can make that will never pass away - and that is our dedication to God. Through that dedication lies eternal life and tomorrow Jesus was going to make that dedication possible.

People came early in the morning

Jesus paused, and looked up and saw. He saw people around him listening to all that he said. They were listening to his words of hope, listening to the way that he dealt with the opposition from the Pharisees and others who had confronted him (in chapter twenty). And now they were listening to what was to come, listening to signs indicating the end of the age. All this would happen one day - but what about now? We might talk about what is to happen in the future but how do we deal with the present? What about the challenges that we have to face today? The world will one day pass away but right now we have a world and all its problems to live with. So Jesus gave another promise:

> But make up your mind not to worry beforehand how you will defend yourselves. For I will give you words and wisdom that none of your adversaries will be able to resist or contradict. (Luke 21:14,15)

We have to live in a world that at times seems to shudder under our feet, a world of betrayal, a world that hems us in from all sides, a world that tramples on all our aspirations and drowns us with its incessant demands. But for those dedicated to God, Jesus promises the ability to come through challenges in the same way as he overcame the opposition that constantly faced him. He promises us the ability to come through whatever is facing us right now.

So Jesus came and taught the people these truths each morning. Each morning he made the short journey from the Mount of Olives down the road that he used on his triumphal entry into the city and into the Temple. It is like a microcosm of God coming from heaven (the Mount of Olives) into the world (Jerusalem) and to us (the Temple). There, early every morning, people came and met with him. They would come and spend the day there just to listen to him. They saw nothing that could be more important and they were right. There was nothing more important than finding God in the world.

But even this was about to pass away. Tomorrow they would come and he would not be there. They would wait, wondering why he was late and, disappointed, some would turn away and go home. Others would stay until late into the evening, until they heard the news that Jesus had been arrested. In the darkness they too went home, shaking their heads. 'All good things must come to an end, I suppose'. 'You can't depend on anybody these days.'

It is just the same now for all who wonder where God is in their troubles. We groan inwardly, and feel the earth shake beneath our feet. We take a sharp breath whilst confronting all that surrounds us as we wonder 'where are you, God?' What we may not realise is that God is working out his purposes in ways that we simply cannot imagine.

Jesus did not come to the Temple that morning. He had somewhere else to be. He was on a mission which was to make it possible for us to be with God; and that mission was about to be accomplished. The pause was over.

CHAPTER TWENTY TWO

ARREST

This is my body, given for you (Luke 22:19)

The arrest of Jesus was planned down to the last detail. What made it so different from other arrests was that the arresting officers did not do the planning. The whole thing was planned by the person being arrested and what makes the event truly unique is that Jesus planned the arrest knowing that it would lead to an excruciatingly painful form of execution. The chief priests and the teachers of the law may have been 'looking for some way to get rid of Jesus' (Luke 22:2), but truth to tell, they didn't have an idea in their collective minds how this was to be achieved – until Judas Iscariot turned up.

In chapter twenty two of Luke's gospel we read that:

> Jesus planned the last supper he had with his disciples.
> He knew that Peter would deny him and that Judas would betray him.
> He returned to the Mount of Olives, where his arrest took place.
> His ordeal started with savage beating and mocking.
> The night finished with the 'trials' before the Jewish elders, then before Herod and before Pilate.

Planning

Jesus not only planned his own arrest, he planned everything else, including the last supper. 'I have eagerly desired to eat this Passover with you before I suffer,' he said, having planned the occasion (Luke 22:15). He knew that Judas would betray him, that Peter would deny him and that all this would ultimately lead to his crucifixion with all the pain and humiliation that would bring. As an example of the detail of his planning, we might look at the man with the water jar, who Luke writes about at the beginning of the chapter.

Jesus told Peter and John to go and prepare a place to eat to celebrate the Passover. The two disciples wanted more detail, so they asked 'where do you want us to prepare for it?' (Luke 22:9). Jesus told them to go into Jerusalem and told them that as they entered it, they would find a man carrying a water jar, who would guide them to the house where they would celebrate the Passover for the last time. We read that the disciples went and - surprise surprise - 'they found things as Jesus had told them' (Luke 22:13).

All this points us to the conclusion that Jesus had set the whole thing up. At some time previously Jesus, knowing all that was to happen to him, had found the house with an upper room in Jerusalem where he would eat this last supper with his disciples. Furthermore, he had found the man who would guide them to this upper room. Just imagine the conversation that Jesus had with this man before all this happened. Let's call him Rob.

Jesus: Rob!
Rob: Yes master?
Jesus: I want you to do something for me.
Rob: Anything you ask, master.
Jesus: What I need you to do is really quite important. Are you ready for it?
Rob: I'm ready, master.
Jesus: Rob, do you know Peter and John?
Rob: I've heard of them, master...
Jesus: Would you be able to recognise them?
Rob: I don't think so, master.
Jesus: OK. Now listen carefully. They're going to arrive in Jerusalem on the Thursday before Passover, and you must be sure that you're at the city gate to meet them. Take them to the house where I"m going to celebrate the Passover with them. Got it?
Rob: When, master?
Jesus: When what?
Rob: When will they arrive, master?
Jesus: I told you – on the Thursday before Passover.
Rob: No, I mean what time on that Thursday?
Jesus: They will arrive anytime before nightfall.

Rob:	But I won't be able to recognise them!
Jesus:	Yes, I've thought of that. You must carry a water jar with you. You must carry the water jar very obviously, and in that way they will know who you are.
Rob:	Women carry water jars, master – not men.
Jesus:	That's precisely it, Rob. That's how they will recognise you. You will be the only man carrying a water jar.
Rob:	Okay. So if I have got this right, master, you want me to stand by the city gate all day on the Thursday before Passover waiting for Peter and John.
Jesus:	That's right Rob!
Rob:	All day I stand there, very obviously carrying a water jar – just like a woman.
Jesus:	You've got it, Rob!
Rob:	And I just stand there looking like a...er...I just stand there until they arrive.
Jesus:	Yep!
Rob:	With lots and lots of people looking at me...with a water jar.
Jesus:	I didn't say that it would be easy, Rob. Are you up for it?
Rob:	Er...yes, master...
Jesus:	You sure?
Rob:	Yes, master.
Jesus:	I'm depending on you.
Rob:	Yes, master.

This story holds two lessons for us. Firstly, if Jesus was prepared to plan to the last detail, then we should do the same. I believe that God honours our planning if we honour God with our planning. In other words, we should plan what we do to the last detail - but we must not leave God out. We should depend on God for every step along the way, because we will need him - particularly if things don't quite go according to our plans.

The second important lesson that the story of the man with a water jug holds for us is about the purpose that God has for us – the role that we are to play in his plan. We might think of ourselves in the 'starring' role – a sort of Peter or John role - or perhaps we might think of ourselves quite differently. We might think that we are ready to serve God in any capacity he asks us to; but, when it comes to it, we might have difficulty coming to terms with what he wants us to do. Serving God in his plan takes humility.

Jesus had planned his last moments with his disciples before his resurrection. Jesus had planned his arrest, trial and crucifixion - and was now ready to go.

Betrayal and denial

He gathered them around the supper table at the Passover. He took the cup of wine and gave thanks:

> *Take this and divide it among you. For I tell you I will not drink again of the fruit of the vine until the Kingdom of God comes.*
> *(Luke 22:17,18)*

The disciples started to become uncertain. They recollected how he had previously talked about his suffering. They recollected the conversation that they had had with him when he told them that he would go to Jerusalem and there he would suffer and be killed. So they tried to put that behind them. It was, after all, Jesus in one of his more morose moments. He didn't really mean it, did he? But Jesus hadn't finished.

> *He took bread, he gave thanks, and broke it, and gave it to them saying 'this is my body given for you, do this in remembrance of me'.*
> *In the same way after supper, he took the cup, saying 'This cup is the new covenant in my blood, which is poured out for you'*
> *(Luke 22:19,20)*

This was to be the basis of their worship from then on, but they didn't realise it then. He then went on to tell them that someone at table with them all was about to betray him. It was all rather unsettling. In fact it was downright exhausting.

They coped with it the best they could. During supper they covered up their confusion and stress, and played silly games amongst themselves. These were typical of the sort of games that men play when they feel up against it. The first game was called 'Top Banana' as they debated as to who was going to get the best jobs after the revolution. The second game that they played was called 'Bravado' as they competed their good intentions and displayed their spiritual muscle power. Peter was particularly good at this game. He stood before them all and proclaimed to Jesus 'I am ready to go with you to prison and to death' (Luke 22:33). Hoorah!

Jesus looked at Peter sorrowfully as he told him that he would deny him three times before the cock crowed the following morning.

The bravado game dragged on. Another disciple attempted to outdo Peter by producing two swords. But Jesus had had enough and got up from the table. The last supper was over, and he walked out into the darkness and back up to the Mount of Olives.

Arrest

The arrest of Jesus was a defining moment. It separated him from everybody else, because they did not expect him to be arrested. The only person who knew what was happening and who was in control of events was Jesus. Those who followed Jesus, particularly the disciples, thought they knew their own minds but ironically none of them did. Peter had no idea that he was about to deny Jesus, any more than Judas had any idea that he would betray him before he came to Jerusalem, and it is wrong for any of us to think that we would have done any better had we been there. We would have been just as confused.

They were exhausted with sorrow about themselves. Things were just not going according to their plans. Jesus, they thought, was about to lead them victorious against all their enemies, against the oppressors - whether the Jewish leaders or the Romans. Exhausted as they were, it must have been a terrible shock to see their friend Judas leading the temple guards out to arrest Jesus. Time to get up! Time to fight! The swords were unsheathed. One of them lunged at a guard and victoriously drew first blood. The revolution had begun.

But then Jesus stepped in. Instead of destroying the arresting party, he told them to put the swords away. Instead of fighting his way out, he healed the guard who had been given a head wound. 'No more of this!' he shouted 'Am I leading a rebellion?' (Luke 22:51,52).

That was it. They had had enough. The disciples bolted into the darkness. Jesus had been betrayed, but the disciples also felt betrayed. They had committed their lives to him and they felt that he had let them down.

From devotion to condemnation

Blessed is the King who comes in the name of the Lord!
(Luke 19:38)

They had shouted their praises as they came down from the Mount of Olives in triumph. 'Peace to heaven and glory in the highest!'

I have often wondered how it was that this passionate cheering crowd, praising their King, could turn in just a few days into a jeering mob chanting for his blood. What happened? In fact the change was wrought not just in a few days but actually in a few hours, in the reaction of disappointed people coming to terms with something that, to their minds, was not working out in the way that they expected. It is incredible how devotion can spiral down to condemnation in such a short time - like a parachutist in freefall. If we look and see how Luke records the events that followed the arrest, we can see this steep slide developing in the people who surrounded Jesus at his arrest.

- **Stage one: Devotion without reciprocation breaks trust.**

  'Lord, I am ready to go with you to prison and to death,' (Luke 22:33) said Peter manfully to Jesus. He meant it as much as a bridegroom swears undying love and devotion for his bride. Peter, not unexpectedly, would have expected that same devotion back. The arrest changed all that as Jesus just let himself be taken. How can one be devoted to someone who seems to throw in the towel? Trust was lost.

- **Stage two: Broken trust forms distance, and distance brings isolation.**

  Peter followed at a distance (Luke 22:54). Peter had fled, the bonds of trust had been broken and he was now apart and distant from Jesus. What Peter didn't understand was that Jesus was doing something that only he could do. In John's gospel we can see how this distance developed.

Peter:	Where are you going?
Jesus:	Where I am going you cannot follow now, but you will follow later
Peter:	Why can't I follow you now? I will lay my life down for you!
Jesus:	Will you really lay down your life for me? I tell you the truth, before the cock crows, you will disown me three times.

(Adapted from John 13:36-38)

- **Stage three: Isolation breeds the need for acceptance and can cause denial**

They had kindled a fire in the middle of the courtyard and had sat down together. Peter sat down with them (Luke 22:55). With the bonds of trust broken and a distance formed between them, Peter felt isolated. He felt deprived of the love of Jesus and was literally out in the cold and on his own. What he most wanted in his misery was warmth – not just from a fire but also from the company of others. But the group around the fire did not have the relationship that Peter had with Jesus. Distanced from Jesus, he needed to be at one with those who didn't know him.

> Do you know Jesus?
> No!
> Are you sure?
> Yes!
> I'm sure you do.
> I don't!
> (Adapted from Luke 22:56-60)

- **Stage four: Denial leads to guilt and pain.**

The cock crowed and the Lord turned and looked straight at Peter (Luke 22:61). Jesus' prediction was sadly right. But how was it possible for Jesus to turn and look at Peter at that dreadful moment of denial? Luke records that Jesus had been taken into the house of the High Priest whilst Peter was distanced from him outside in the courtyard. However, when the cock crowed, Peter felt the eyes of Jesus on him and recollected all that Jesus had predicted. It was the type of terrible self-revelation that we all dread. This was probably the worst moment of Peter's life.

- **Stage five: Dealing with pain through mocking and beating.**

The men who were guarding Jesus began mocking and beating him (Luke 22:63). The soldiers were enjoying making someone's life very miserable. Jesus had done nothing to hurt them, but a good bit of mocking and beating took their mind away from their own misery. Mocking a lost devotion brings temporary relief. In various ways we 'beat up' others, particularly those we love, with a perception that they are to blame rather than accept any error on our part.

- **Stage six: crucify him! Crucify him!**

That day, Herod and Pilate became friends, where before they had been enemies (Luke 23:12). Both Herod and Pilate had no particular desire to order the execution of Jesus. They saw him as no threat. We read in John's gospel that Pilate tried to set Jesus free (John 19:12). Luke records in the next chapter (chapter 23) that Herod wanted to see Jesus perform a miracle. Herod and Pilate had a common purpose, but were both to be disappointed. Like the disciples on the Mount of Olives they also had that sense of betrayal from the man that they were trying to help. Oh, to hell with him then! I only wanted to see if he was for real. He means nothing to us! Crucify him! Crucify him!

Praise to condemnation in just six short stages that took only a few hours to complete.

Brokenness

It is only recently that I have been able to glimpse the depths of Jesus brokenness when he was arrested. It was bad enough that he was betrayed by one of his closest followers but worse still was the fact that he knew his disciples felt he had let them down. There was no way that he could communicate to them an understanding of what he had to do.

He had told them all straight what was to happen, but it was incomprehensible to them. Nobody at the time was able to understand that, to achieve the impossible, to reunite them - and us - with God, he was going to have to die. The brokenness of his body on the cross was to display the brokenness of his heart as he saw the disappointment and confusion of all around him.

> *He took the bread, gave thanks and broke it and gave it to them saying 'this is my body given for you; do this in remembrance of me.' (Luke 22:19)*

They didn't understand then, but after tomorrow they would begin to understand. And when they understood they would remember the moment when he broke the bread at the last supper.

CHAPTER TWENTY THREE

PARADISE

...today you will be with me in paradise (Luke 23:43)

We are surrounded by people who are baying, laughing and taunting and we are naked - not a stitch on. We try to cover our nakedness, to cover our shame but we find that we can't move and all the time our naked body is racked with pain. This is a nightmare, our worst nightmare. It was Jesus' nightmare at the Place of the Skull.

Since the day his ministry began back in Galilee, Jesus had always been surrounded by people and it was no different now. On this day, the day that he was crucified, he was surrounded by rulers who questioned him, by teachers of the law who accused and ridiculed him, by soldiers who beat him within an inch of his life and by a crowd who, with one voice, demanded his death.

> Crucify him! Crucify him! Release us Barrabas. Come on, It's our right at the Passover festival to give us someone and we want Barrabas. Good old Barrabas! At least he does what he says. He will lead us against our enemies not like this other complete waste of time. Crucify him!
> (Adapted from Luke 23:18-20)

They raged around Jesus, a crowd venting its fury at the unfairness that afflicted their lives; and Jesus said little to them for he knew what he had to do, and understood their disappointment that he wasn't doing what they had expected. With one voice they condemned him, because with one mind they could not understand that he was about to achieve the impossible for them.

So he began to walk on a road out of Jerusalem under the cross, with its crushing weight on his back, already striped with blood from the beating that he had received from the soldiers. Up in front were two criminals also to be crucified that day. No one knows now what they did wrong and most people then wouldn't have known either, but whatever it was, they too were condemned. But progress was slow – too slow. Jesus couldn't keep up. The beating had been severe – too severe. So the soldiers commandeered someone from the crowd to carry the cross.

And now at the Place of the Skull, surrounded still, he was tied and nailed hand and foot to the cross with one of the criminals on his left side and the other on his right.

The left side criminal

The criminal that we will see crucified on the left of Jesus prayed a prayer to him. It was the prayer of a man in deep anguish and agonising pain. It's a prayer that many have prayed at times of deep distress, whether or not they believe in God:

Aren't you the Messiah? Save yourself and us! (Luke 23:39)

Jesus what's happening? What are you doing? I'm in a crisis and you are not much help. If you are the God of love, how can you let this happen? If you are God Almighty then show yourself! Do something about my troubles! But you don't seem to care. I get no answers from you.

The left side criminal railed against Jesus. He did get an answer, but not from where he expected it. It was the right side criminal who answered him.

The right side criminal

How many times in our lives do we find our demanding prayers answered by someone who also has huge problems? The criminal on the right side of Jesus, racked in just as much pain, answered the complaint:

Don't you fear God'...'since you are under the same sentence? We are punished justly, for we are getting what our deeds deserve. But this man has done nothing wrong. (Luke 23:40)

I have ranted my frustrations at God many times in my life. I don't think that ranting against God has ever got me closer to any answers, other than allowing me to let off steam. This is not altogether a bad thing, but that's as far as it goes. Our first instinct, when we come against a problem or face a disaster, is often to blame God - or anybody other than ourselves. Yet, if we are honest, much of the mess we are in is often of our own making and this is what the right side criminal realised.

Actually he realised three things. First he realised the truth about himself. He had done much that was wrong. He realised what he was and that he could do nothing to help himself. He was both helpless before God and within himself. Secondly, he realised that the man in the middle was very different, and that ranting at him was neither justified nor useful. These two realisations are unremarkable in themselves but it was his third realisation that was nothing short of a miracle.

Jesus, remember me when you come into your kingdom
(Luke 23:42)

He knew Jesus. He called him by name. Perhaps he had met Jesus at some point on the road into Jerusalem; but he had enough knowledge of him to know that there was something special about him. Yet here he was, this same Jesus, nailed up on a cross and apparently as helpless as he was. They were both soon to die. Asphyxiation would kill them when they became too exhausted to breathe any more. So in this undeniably hopeless situation we have one dying man asking another dying man to remember him!

What the right side criminal saw, in that insightful moment, was that Jesus was much more than a man dying on a cross. This might have been the last day on earth for the right sided criminal but, in his moment of lucidity, he saw that this was not the end for Jesus. This Jesus would be able to remember him 'when he came into his kingdom'. Incredible insight deserves an incredible reply and that is what the right side criminal got from Jesus. It was this reply that changed him but it also changed all humanity.

Truly, I tell you, today you will be with me in paradise. (Luke 23:43)

This conversation only makes sense if we realise that Jesus was in the process of achieving the impossible. He was about to make it possible for this criminal to be with him in paradise. He was about to make it possible for him to be reconciled to God and to inherit eternal life. How did that happen?

Luke writes that darkness now covered the land, and Jesus called out 'Father, into your hands I commit my spirit' (Luke 23:46). In this terrible darkness in the middle of the day, Jesus achieved what he came to do.

The impossible achieved

What happened at the Place of the Skull where three men were crucified in the darkness? How did Jesus achieve the impossible by dying a criminal's death on a wooden cross? We have to remind ourselves that there is something huge between us and God. It is a gulf so wide that no man can cross. What separates us from God is sin.

Our problem with God is sin

If God is God, then he is the creator of all there is. He is the creator of the universe and we are specks on a minor planet in His universe. A relationship between such diverse opposites is inconceivable. John the Baptist, the forerunner of Jesus, recognised this when he said that 'one more powerful than I will come, the thongs of whose sandals I am not worthy to untie,' (Luke 3:16). John voiced what many have said since - a recognition of the huge gap that divides God from us. A recognition of sin.

God's problem with us is sin

There is a huge difference between what God is and what we have become. God wants two things from us. He wants us to worship Him and he wants us to love and honour each other. Instead God sees that we worship the gods of wealth and power – the same gods that tempted him in the wilderness in Luke chapter four. There is strife between nations, breakdown of the environment and poverty afflicting much of the world. Communities and religions strive against each other in wars and feuds, losing all sense of love, honour and respect for each other. But closer to home, it is evidenced in the strife that afflicts families, the workplace and the church. And closer still, it is evidenced within each of us as we strive to obtain more and more. This huge gap divides God from us. It is my belief that this is God's recognition of sin. We might continue with the graphic illustration of this:

GOD ⊣S|N⊢ US

However there is no gap between Jesus and God. Jesus had no problems with the creator God because he was the Son of God – God in this world. Likewise God has no problem with Jesus because everything about Jesus was pure. God said of Jesus 'You are my son whom I love, with you I am well pleased' (Luke 3:22). Therefore there is no sin that divides Jesus from God.

GOD ————— JESUS

The impossible was achieved in the middle of the day when darkness fell on Jesus hanging on the cross, as it fell on everybody around the cross then and ever since. The darkness represented sin, our sin, everything that divides us from God. At that moment the darkness of sin that separates us from God was placed on Jesus. The sin that is ours was now on him and then he died and our sin died with him.

Nothing separated Jesus from God and now, bearing our sin, he bridged the gap of sin that divided God from us.

GOD ⊣JESUS⊢ US

Jesus, remember me.

Today you will be with me in paradise.

The words Jesus said to the right side criminal are the same words that will be said to all who say 'Jesus, remember me'. We will still get it wrong - sometimes badly wrong - but we are now able to take whatever is wrong to Jesus, who carried our sin. The path to God was opened at the cross and it will never be closed.

What is so incredible is that God did this. He had so much love for us that he came as Jesus into our world to take on everything that separated us from Him. We are his creation, and he loves us as a Father loves his child. In an enlightened moment, a dying criminal got a glimpse of just that. In the darkness there at the Place of the Skull, the impossible was achieved.

The first member of the church of Jesus

Who was the first member of the church of Jesus? Who was the first person to benefit from Jesus achieving the impossible? Who was the first to enter the presence of God through the death of Jesus on the cross? Was it his mother Mary? Maybe it was Peter once he had overcome the misery of his denial? Or maybe it was John whom 'Jesus loved'? No it was none of these people.

The first member of the church of Jesus Christ was a criminal!

Jesus said to the right side criminal, 'today you will be with me in paradise'. Jesus had never said anything like this to anyone before. The moment that this criminal asked Jesus to remember him was the moment when the first human crossed that huge gap that separated us from God. At that moment he, a criminal, was reconciled to God. He was in paradise because Jesus died for him.

Two days later, Jesus would say something similar to Peter, who would be the rock on which the church was founded, but right now Peter and all the other disciples were far away in the distance. He would say the same to the women who were nearby but who, at that moment, didn't understand. And there is a day that has either happened or is to come, when the same words might be said to us. It will happen when we say 'Jesus, remember me'. On that day, Jesus will turn to us and tell us that paradise is ours as well.

But for now the church of Jesus had just one member and he was a convicted criminal.

Darkness

It was dark over the Place of the Skull, so dark, dark as soot. There are times in our lives when darkness prevails. Times when we simply can't see what is going on within and around us, as we blindly stumble around looking for God, who we cannot find. This was the darkness that Jesus entered while he hung on the cross.

His broken body was not only despised by those surrounding him – those who did not understand what he was doing. It was even worse. As always, Jesus looked for God, and as he groped through the darkness of his mind for God he could not find him. For the first time, God was not there. God had switched out the lights and gone away, leaving Jesus alone to carry all that separates us from God. It was because of this supreme sacrifice that the church of Jesus had one member.

Jesus was born in darkness and he died in darkness and, as he died, through the darkness came a loud cry. He knew that God had left him, yet even in his despair he cried out in confidence 'Father into your hands I commit my spirit' (Luke 23:46). In this darkness, Jesus knew that his spirit was safe in God's hands and that his work was completed.

It was at this point that the church of Jesus doubled.

The centurion in charge of the crucifixion party was close by - much closer than the disciples, who were still far away. He was a hardened man, just as many of us have been hardened by life's experiences. Yet he came to a stark realisation. 'Surely this was a righteous man,' he said (Luke 23:47). In Mark's version of the gospel account, the centurion said 'Surely this man was the Son of God,' (Luke 15:39). This exclamation was more than an expression of 'not guilty'. This was very much the same sort of admission that was made by the right side criminal and so, effectively, the same promise applied to the centurion as well. The centurion had found the way to paradise as he scrambled at that moment into the kingdom of heaven.

Then out of the darkness came a third man. His name was Joseph of Arimathea – another Joseph. The first Joseph was there in the darkness of the stable at his birth, and the second Joseph came out of the darkness at his death. The first protected the infant Jesus after his birth and the second buried his body after his death. This Joseph of Arimathea was a member of the council that had condemned Jesus but he had not 'consented to their decision or action' (Luke 23:51). At considerable risk to himself, he went to Pilate and asked for the body so that he might bury it.

And so the church of Jesus grew to three.

The church of Jesus had been born, and it was the end of the first day of its life. When that day finished, the church of Jesus had three members. One of them was a convicted criminal, another had crucified him and the third was a member of the Council that had
condemned him. All three had found Jesus in different ways as we find Jesus in different ways.

So for any who believe that they are beyond the reach of God – look at the first three members of the church of Jesus. The church of Jesus is open to all. Let no one, least of all the church, ever forget this.

Today you will be with me in paradise

'Today you will be with me in paradise'. How can these words be said to us, for us? The answer is by our taking the same three steps as the first member of the church of Jesus – the right side criminal who died with him. This is his prayer – perhaps we can pray it as well:

Recognising ourselves: Jesus, I recognise that there is much that separates me from God.

Recognising Jesus: Jesus, there is nothing that separates you from God.

And the acknowledgment
of our helplessness: Jesus, remember me in your kingdom.

Now be assured that the same words are said to us. 'Today you will be with me in paradise'. So, was Jesus' death on the cross the end of it? By no means, for something just as incredible was to come.

CHAPTER TWENTY FOUR

EASTER DAY

Were not our hearts burning within us while he talked with us
(Luke 24:32)

It was the first Easter Day. Inside the tomb it was pitch black but on that first Easter Day, Jesus got up from the darkness and went out into the light.

Jesus was alive!

Jesus' itinerary on that first Easter Day was amazing, bearing in mind that he had been crucified two days before. In Luke's gospel, in chapter twenty-four, Luke records

Early morning:	Jesus rose up from the tomb and walked past the stone that had been rolled away and out into the world that had killed him.
Later morning:	He met with Peter in the vicinity of Jerusalem.
Afternoon:	He met with two men on the road to a village called Emmaus lying seven miles out of Jerusalem. When they reached Emmaus, Jesus stayed and had tea with them before getting back to Jerusalem.
That evening:	Back in Jerusalem he met the disciples and stayed and ate a late supper.
Into the night:	Jesus taught his disciples so that they could begin to understand what had happened and what they were to do.

This was the itinerary of a very healthy man. Doctor Luke would have been impressed! Let us look at the events of that day a little more closely.

Early morning: looking in the wrong place

It was early morning on the first day of the week when the women went to the tomb and found the stone rolled away and the body of Jesus gone. Unsurprisingly the women wondered what had happened, and began to search for his body. We might imagine them outside in the garden searching, and thinking that someone had taken him, echoing the searches for him at the beginning of Jesus' life (see chapter two). The women at the tomb searched for Jesus but didn't find him - for he was not dead.

Gospel accounts differ as to what happened then, and I don't think we should be particularly surprised at this, given the confusion of the moment. Luke records that there were two men at the tomb. Luke describes these two as having clothes that gleamed like lightning (Luke 24:4). They had a message for the women.

> Why do you look for the living among the dead? He is not here; he has risen! Remember how he told you, while he was still with you in Galilee. The Son of Man must be delivered into the hands of sinners, be crucified and on the third day be raised again.
> (Luke 24:5-6)

But who were these two men who told them that they were searching in the wrong place? The women clearly thought that they were angels, as Luke makes that clear later in the chapter; but 'angels' might sound fanciful to some. Who is to say that the women didn't see angels?

We shouldn't let this get in the way of understanding what happened that day. Some would have no difficulty with this but others would be more sceptical.

For the sceptics then, here is a story of an experience which I think might be shared by many others. I was in church listening to a talk. It doesn't matter that it was in church – it might have been anywhere. In the course of the talk, the man who was speaking used a short phrase and, as soon as I heard what he said, I had the answer to a question that I had struggled with for some years. It was like a great beam of light pouring through me. The penny had dropped with a mighty clang! I wanted to get up and shout 'I understand!', but out of respect for the speaker I remained quiet. And the speaker? Martin is about six foot tall and built like a blockhouse yet for me that morning, he was an angel sent by God!

Later morning: wondering and not believing

Breathlessly the women came back from the tomb, bursting to tell the others what was happening. But the reception they received was far from cosy. They did not believe the women, because their words seemed to them like nonsense (Luke 24:11). After that day of crucifixion, who could blame them for being so dismissive? Nevertheless, it must have been very frustrating for the women. At that point the women had at least some understanding of what Jesus had done, but the men had not. But Peter couldn't let it stay that way. He had to go and see for himself. Peter ran for all he was worth and seeing the strips of linen, he began to wonder what had happened.

Now at that point in chapter twenty four, Luke appears to do something rather curious. Instead of staying with Peter and seeing what happened to him next, he switches the account to two other men walking out of Jerusalem to a village seven miles away called Emmaus. At first glance the account doesn't seem to flow. Why doesn't Luke stay with Peter? After all, toward the end of the chapter we read that Peter did meet with the risen Jesus later that morning; but Luke tells us nothing of how that happened. Instead our attention is turned to how the risen Jesus met with two other men.

As I see it, the whole point of Luke chapter twenty-four is about the risen Jesus. The women, Peter, the disciples and the two men on the road are purely incidental. We will understand it better if we read this chapter as a day in the life of Jesus after he had risen.

Afternoon: burning within us

Sometime toward noon that day, two men set out for Emmaus. One of the men was called Cleopas and we know nothing about the other man. We know the approximate time that they set out, because they had heard the women's story but not about Peter's subsequent encounter with Jesus. Like everyone else, they didn't believe the women. I get the impression that they weren't walking fast – more of a slump-shouldered shuffle as they chewed over the events and their disappointment. As a result they arrived at their destination just before evening.

However, on the road they met Jesus - who they didn't recognise. 'Were not our hearts burning within us while he talked to us on the road?' they said (Luke 24:32), yet they still didn't recognise him. Was it really Jesus? If it was, why didn't they recognise him?

But isn't it obvious? Consider for a minute. Have we not at times been somewhere - perhaps a supermarket or a street - and seen someone who looks like somebody that we once knew? There's a moment of recognition but then we recall that the loved person, who we thought we had recognised, has in fact died. For a painful moment we are reminded of the grief that we suffered and suffer still. We turn away and look no more. Isn't that what happened? To those two men, Jesus was dead. The man who had joined them in their amble to Emmaus might have looked like Jesus but it couldn't possibly be him, could it? Until...

....until he did something that meant that it could only be him. They were at table, where they had invited him to stay, and there he broke bread in a way that only he broke bread. Another penny dropped with a great clang and Jesus left them with their emotion. They were probably a little shocked that somehow he disappeared (Luke 24:31), but Jesus knew that they would want to hang on to him. He also knew that he had to get back to the disciples in Jerusalem. So he left quickly. The two men would see him again in a few hours.

That evening: it is true! He is risen!

As Jesus expected, Cleopas and his companion hot-footed it back to Jerusalem. It had taken them several hours to amble over the seven miles to Emmaus, but it took them half the time to get back. What kind of reception were they going to get, they wondered? After all, the women didn't get the kind of welcome they wanted when they got back from the tomb. Could they expect any better?

They need not have feared. Jesus had been at work. That morning, before they set out for Emmaus, he had appeared to Simon Peter. So when the two men arrived back in Jerusalem they were not treated with ridicule but with joy. It's true! The Lord has risen and appeared to Simon! (Luke 24:34)

And then...

While they were still talking about this, Jesus himself stood among them and said to them 'Peace be with you' (Luke 24:36)

Oh what I would give to have been in that room at that moment! I wonder how Jesus got in? Possibly with the sandwiches – who knows? But it is not difficult to imagine the look of frozen disbelief that spread across each face when they saw him. They thought that they had seen a ghost! 'Peace be with you,' said Jesus to the disciples, and they needed peace right then. Unlike the two men at Emmaus, they recognised Jesus instantly because they had the testimonies of the women, Peter, Cleopas and his companion. So there was already an air of anticipation when Jesus stood among them in the room. We can only imagine what was racing through their minds at that moment. Was Jesus truly alive? Could they trust their own eyes?

Why are you troubled, and why do doubts rise in your minds? Look at my hands and my feet. It is I myself! Touch me and see; a ghost does not have flesh and bones, as you see I have. (Luke 24:38-39)

I am imagining that room with those disciples looking in disbelief at Jesus. I can just see them timidly prodding him, poking fingers into his back and tummy looking askance at his hands and feet. And then Jesus said something that settled all questions-marks and made them laugh at the same time.

'I'm hungry!' he said. (Luke 24:41). How many times had they heard that before! Luke goes out of his way to tell us what the risen Jesus was like. Yes, the doctor diagnosed, Jesus was alive and in strapping health and, yes, he was still in the same body that was crucified.

Into the night: explanation

It was time to settle down. On the road to Jerusalem, it had been difficult for Jesus to get the disciples to understand what his mission was about. He had tried but their minds were fixed elsewhere. But now it was different. Because he was alive they began to see that Jesus had achieved what no one else could have done. So they all calmed down and he began to explain things to them:

The Messiah will suffer and rise from the dead on the third day, and repentance for the forgiveness of sins will be preached in his name to all nations (Luke 24:46-47)

Jesus was going back to his Father in heaven. Long into the night the disciples listened to what they were to do. They were to preach the forgiveness of sins. They were to be the ones who would do the explaining now. They would tell people how his death on the cross had bridged the vast gap between us and God. They would explain to everybody they met that, through the cross, nothing can separate us from God. This was their message for all nations.

But it wouldn't be plain sailing, and many difficulties would be encountered. The twelve disciples remembered the hash they made of things when they were sent out by Jesus on the road (chapter ten). Only later did they begin to understand how reliant they were on Jesus, so Jesus told them that they 'would be clothed with power from on high' (Luke 24:49). It was a promise that would be delivered with mighty force at the Feast of Pentecost in a few weeks time. The Spirit of Jesus, through this small group, would take the message of Jesus into an unknowing world.

The road to the impossible

We have reached the end of the gospel of Luke. Our journey through the gospel will have been a different experience for each of us, just as it was for the women, Peter, the two men on the road to Emmaus and the disciples. If we have a mind to find Jesus as they did, then we might expect times when we will look in the wrong place as the women did after they found the body had gone. There will also be times when we won't believe, just as the disciples initially disbelieved when they were told that Jesus had risen. There will be times of wondering as Peter wondered when he left the empty tomb. There will be times when we will ask questions but find that we need God to lead us to answers. There will be times when we will find answers because our hearts will burn within us.

But in the end it all comes down to a personal encounter with Jesus. Earlier this year, my brother-in-law was at the side of a dying man, someone he knew. The man realised he was dying, and in these final moments of life, all verbal communication had gone. A squeeze of a hand was all that was left. The conversation that my brother-in- law had went something like this.

> Tony, do you want to be certain about where you are going?
> (Squeeze of hand)
> The gospel tells us that we can call on Jesus and he will take us to be with him. Would you like me to pray this for you?
> (Squeeze of hand)
> Tony, receive his peace

It was only possible for my brother-in-law to say this because of what Jesus did on the cross when he opened the path to God and bridged the gap of sin.

Today you will be with me in paradise

Those in the world who have encountered Jesus have a job to do. We are to tell the nations. That won't be easy and at times it will trouble us and possibly cause anguish; but it is the most important message we can convey to anyone, whether they are full of life or on their deathbed. Jesus comes to us with the same message that he had for his disciples as they gathered together in Jerusalem. 'Peace be with you,' he said to them - and with that same peace we are able to go out into the darkness of the world with Easter Day in our hearts. We will need the Spirit of Jesus to enable us to take the message of Jesus to others. It is the same spirit of Jesus that first came at Pentecost.

EPILOGUE

PENTECOST

'What on earth am I doing here?' he thought, as they hoisted him onto the nearest cart. Simon Peter remembered Jesus' words to them all just before he went to Heaven. 'Wait in Jerusalem until I send the Holy Spirit to you'. (Acts 1:4)

Peter didn't rightly understand what Jesus meant but then there was much that Peter didn't understand about Jesus. However, if that is what Jesus wanted them to do then that is what they would do. So, back in Jerusalem, they had waited and prayed. They didn't have to wait very long. They only had to wait until the Feast of Pentecost.

Suddenly, as they were praying, the house was hit by a whirlwind, or that is how is felt. Fire was everywhere – firing them up. They found themselves with energy inside, which burst them out of the house in the same way that Jesus had burst out of the tomb. Now they were outside, praising God in words that were understood by everybody in cosmopolitan Jerusalem as they crowded round to see what was happening. That's when they hoisted Peter up onto the nearest cart. 'I've never spoken in public before,' thought Peter as he looked over the thousands that surrounded him 'oh well, I suppose there's no better time to start. Here goes!' and he raised his voice:

> People of Israel, listen to this. Jesus of Nazareth was a man accredited by God to you by miracles, wonders and signs... This man was handed over to you by God's deliberate plan and foreknowledge; and you, with the help of wicked men, put him to death by nailing him to the cross. But God raised him from the dead, freeing him from the agony of death, because it was impossible for death to keep its hold of him' (Acts 2:22-24)

When Peter had finished speaking that day, some three thousand people had been added to the church of Jesus.

Nothing is impossible with God.